Helena
The Town and The People

by Tom Palmer

Photography by Rick Graetz

published by
Montana Magazine
Helena, Montana

William A. Cordingley, Chairman
Rick Graetz, President
Mark Thompson,
Director of Publications
Barbara Fifer, Assistant Book Editor
Carolyn Cunningham,
Editor—Montana Magazine

Acknowledgments

Acknowledgments

Thanks to: Dave Walter, research director at the Montana Historical Society, for his direction and encouragement; those nine Helenans who so graciously helped to build a barn at the Lewis and Clark Library on March 23, 1987; Jean Baucus for her generous access to her photo collection; Ray Breuninger for his assistance with the geology of Helena; Rick Graetz; and especially to Teri for her enthusiasm.

Dedication

For Ryan and all those fortunate to have been born in this valley.

About the Author

Tom Palmer, an award-winning former reporter for the Helena *Independent Record,* is a writer who resides in Helena with his wife and son.

Library of Congress Cataloging-in-Publication Information

Palmer, Tom, 1952-
 Helena : the town and the people / by Tom Palmer ; photography by Rick Graetz.
 p.   cm.
Bibliography: p.
ISBN 0-938314-41-6 : $19.95. ISBN 0-938314-32-7 (pbk.) : $13.95
 1. Helena (Mont.)—Description. 2. Helena Region (Mont.)—Description and travel. 3. Helena (Mont.)—Description—Views. 4. Helena Region (Mont.)—Description and travel—Views.
I. Graetz, Rick. II. Title.
F739.H4P345 1987
978.6'615—dc 19   87-28309
                                                 CIP

ISBN 0-938314-32-7 (P)
ISBN 0-938314-41-6 (H)

Design by Linda Collins. Published by Montana Magazine.

Facing page: *The Atlas Block on what was then called Main Street. Atlas, supporting the world on his shoulders, can be seen at third-story level.* MONTANA HISTORICAL SOCIETY

This page, top: *Northern Pacific Railroad depot in December 1885, at the terminus of Helena Avenue; Mt. Helena visible at left.* F. JAY HAYNES PHOTO, MONTANA HISTORICAL SOCIETY

Above: *Aerial view from above the top of Mt. Helena, looking northeast across the city.* TOM CORDINGLEY

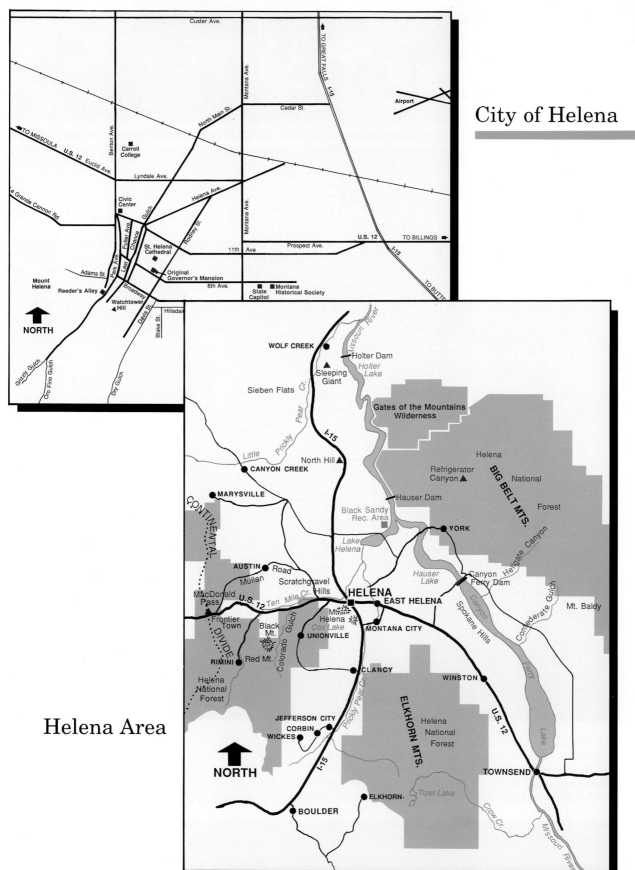

City of Helena

Helena Area

4

Contents

Front cover, top: Downtown Helena from the south;
left: Montana Capitol; center: Anchor Park, Bluestone
House and Firetower; right: Last Chance Gulch
pedestrian mall. RICK GRAETZ PHOTOS
Back cover: Cox Lake, Helena National Forest.
RICK GRAETZ
This page, top: In the Big Belt Mountains. JOHN REDDY
Bottom: Montana Capitol. RICK GRAETZ

1 THIS PLACE

Helena's short official history, that of gold discovery and development, is as easy to follow and as well traveled as any of the Elkhorn trails to Casey Meadows. But to query "Why Helena?" instead of asking what made the town, invites one to use his feelings, his intuitions. The Italian novelist Italo Calvino posed the question magically in *Invisible Cities*. He wrote: "But why does this city exist? What line separates the inside from the outside, the rumble of wheels from the howl of wolves?"

Once you know what has happened in a place it feels different, lends it character and personality. But you have to find the line that separates the inside from the outside in order to make sense of history, in order to make sense of place.

I once was talking with Missoula novelist Jim Welch, Helena novelist and rancher Ralph Beer and rancher Scott Hibbard. We were each set to thinking about "place" and perhaps that line, when Welch, a Blackfeet/Gros Ventre Indian, began telling a story that was centered on a place. The place was the grave site of Malcolm Clarke, located north of Helena on land owned by the Baucus family, up on Sieben Flats. Clarke was killed by his wife's Piegan Blackfeet cousin in 1869, less than five years after discovery of gold in Last Chance Gulch. There was nothing of Helena in July 1864. By August 1869, 3,000 people were here, with buildings and businesses to serve them. The Blackfeet were among the people they were displacing. Hibbard admitted that he seldom paid any mind to Malcolm Clarke's grave and then Welch said the land is covered with the places that hold similar stories that might never be told and certainly will be forgotten be-

The first view of Helena for travelers heading south on Interstate 15 is from North Pass, looking across the Prickly Pear Valley at the capital city snug against mountains. JOHN REDDY

The home that trader Malcolm Clarke built in the 1860s for his family north of the Prickly Pear Valley. It later was used as the Mitchell stage stop.
COURTESY JEAN BAUCUS

cause we have lost our oral story-telling traditions.

If I can't talk to you, I will write you letters, show you photographs, tell you stories about place that you can pass on. No real road map through time, but good side trips on both sides of the line. This text is not an attempt to survey all of Helena history nor to be a file of facts for future researchers. I have discovered things that have interested me about this place and offer some of them for you to read.

Take a side trip. Get into the car and take off. Travel north through the Wolf Creek Canyon, along the Little Prickly Pear Creek, a fine trout stream, and head on up Augusta way. Breathe in the Rocky Mountain Front, stop at a Hutterite colony, buy some bread, a fryer and some potatoes. Watch the land. Continue on. Stop and feel the fence surrounding a nuclear Minuteman missile silo and realize there are often grizzly bears beyond, in the rugged bottoms along the Front. Get a sense of where you are. Stop the car in the middle of the highway. Get out and holler at the mountains. No one will hear you. In Augusta have a beer in the Buckhorn Bar. If you do this during hunting season, remember that this temporarily bustling town is now the hub of the rich hunting grounds with considerable thanks due to the development of Helena and the seclusion of the Bob Marshall Wilderness Area. Now, head back to Helena an hour before sunset, on the same route animals used during their migration to the winter range. Watch for the rough-legged hawks, lifted by thermals, hunting field mice and jackrabbits.

The St. Helena Cathedral of the Roman Catholic Diocese of Helena, which covers western Montana. DARLENE DURGAN

The road you travel follows a trail used by woolly mammoths, the three-toed horses, camels, zebras, buffaloes and even dinosaurs when they roamed Montana's tropical swamps. Used too, by prehistoric people from Asia and later by Blackfeet hunting parties whose travois tracks have been tattooed to the earth by a powerful nation of people drawn along the migratory patterns of buffalo and the sun falling lower, falling farther south. There are still places on the Blackfeet's Old North Trail where you can run your fist through the ruts left by their travois. Put your ear to them. Let your heart beat on them. How are we now to use this land?

You should reach the top of the North Hill at dusk. Helena and her valley will be spread there in the distance— a lake of lights. It shocks you, really. It seems at once to affront and to invite. Affront because the land has lulled you as a baby in a cradle. What lies outside the gates of the city is not so hostile from a car. With the power of speed, blazing over roads tamped by indigenous ungulates and prehistoric hunters, you are the center of a universe that still can appear so wild and primitive and there, suddenly, in the pocket of the valley, sits a city in that dark wilderness.

And it is the city whispering and winking the irony, asking you where you belong. Here or there? In an instant you lose the intoxication of landscape. You are separated from the land in a city, even in a city as small and as remote as Helena.

In the dark, 20th-century men and women can feel what it must have been like for early visitors as they crested the Old North Trail and saw what the Blackfeet Indians called Many-Sharp-Points-Ground. In a later time, and 49 years before the famed and misnamed Four Georgians wearily crossed the valley, William Clark stopped and pulled 17 cactus spines from his feet and called this place the Valley of the Prickly Pear.

In the dark we understand the lights as those who came before understood what the geography promised. A refuge.

And, of course, this place boasted the promise of gold that could be tapped from the mouths of the gulches like loose fillings. Here men squirmed between the muscled hills and sank shaft after shaft all on a promise. That promise brought a far different breed here— unlike any of the others who came before them, unlike some who established richer mining camps—many of these people stayed and created in this place one of the unique cities in the West.

Helena from the South Hills, with busy Montana Avenue in the foreground. MARK THOMPSON

9

2 THE SUMMERTEER TOUR

Sometime in April, visitors begin phoning and writing Helenans. They will be coming west, or to the West, and where is Helena, anyway? By the time a visitor to Helena departs, his host not only has made sure he will for all time remember where Helena is, he has subtly, and maybe unintentionally, spoon-fed his friend local lore and history throughout the visit.

Helenans are summerteers. By the time the Governor's Cup Marathon is run in early June, cabin fever is swept away. The sun rises at 5:30 a.m. and sets 16 hours later. Seldom-seen friends and relatives begin arriving in town for their often too-short visits and upon their arrival most Helenans become something akin to ex-officio representatives of the Chamber of Commerce and the Montana Historical Society.

The love for Helena among Helenans is extraordinary and like perennial flowers it blooms each summer. The town is an easy place to become attached to. The tree-lined streets where mid- to late-20th century homes are bracketed by well-kept Victorian mansions lend the neighborhoods a settled mood, a civilized spirit.

The mood and spirit are moored in the past and the people who live here are anxious to tell the story. What has evolved is pop history, easy to tell and to remember, that captures a moment as if in a photograph.

Click. The "Guardian of the Gulch" fire tower on Watchtower Hill has become the city's logo. Towers have been on the hill since 1868, and Helena was leveled several times by fire. The Guardian of the Gulch, with its watchman's room, was erected after the fire of 1874 engulfed most of the downtown business district. The alarm bell has been removed from the structure, but many long-time Helenans can remember when the bell

Left: *The Park Avenue finish line for the annual Governor's Cup race. Left foreground is the former Eddy Bakery building; center background, the Montana Club; right background, the Power Block.* **Top:** *The restored "Guardian of the Gulch" fire tower above the south end of downtown.*
RICK GRAETZ PHOTOS

tolled the curfew hour for youngsters.

Click. Last Chance Gulch, born and christened on July 14, 1864 by four weary gold prospectors who struck paydirt. "The Gulch," with its ornate buildings along a street conforming to the first mining claims, has managed to retain some of the flavor of Helena's golden era. Once the undisputed financial center of Montana, Helena's Main Street (now Last Chance Gulch) rivaled in free-wheeling grandeur the financial districts of more firmly established eastern cities.

The period was colorful and spirited and the business and commercial buildings reflected Helena's spirit and unbridled optimism. Especially in the business blocks. Some of the more notable golden-era buildings still standing on Last Chance Gulch include the Iron Front Building (1887), Sam Hauser's Romanesque First National Bank (1886), and the Atlas Block (1888)— often described as Helena's most Romantic structure—and the impressive and beautifully

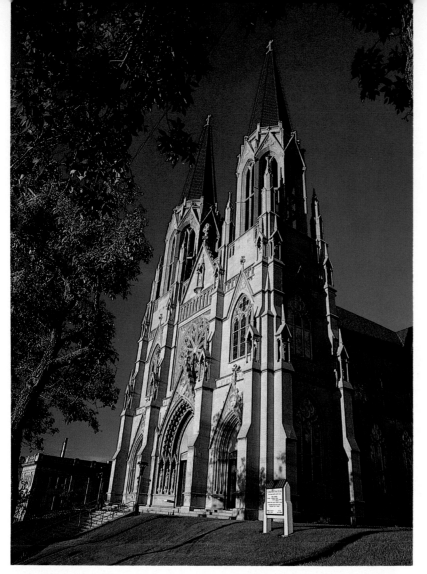

St. Helena Cathedral. The 12-feet-tall golden crosses atop the spires are visible throughout the city.
JOHN REDDY

Votive Church and the Cologne (Germany) Cathedral, resembles the Gothic churches built in Europe during the 12th to 16th centuries. The statues within are carved from Carrara marble, the pews are hand-carved oak and the fixtures are hand-forged bronze. The 46 stained-glass windows were purchased for $750 each from the Munich, Germany artisan F.X. Zettler.

Although the cathedral's main benefactor, the cantankerous Irishman Thomas Cruse, was present at the first mass held in the basement on November 8, 1914, he died five days before the cathedral's official dedication on Christmas Day 1914. Cruse is entombed in the elaborate mausoleum that dominates Resurrection Cemetery north of Helena.

Click. Helena's Civic Center was built in 1921 as the town's Algeria Shrine Temple and, typical of Helena's overstated sense of competition with the rest of the world, someone ranked its size as the 10th largest auditorium in the world and counted the 1 million bricks laid during con-

restored Power Block (1888) that stands at the corner of Last Chance Gulch and Sixth Avenue.

In the 1960s, Helena's downtown was a depressing sight. With the help of more than $13 million from the federal Model Cities and Urban Renewal program, 228 build-

ings were razed and hundreds of businesses and families were displaced. There is no question that the gulch is now in better condition, but many still believe that the urban renewal tornado wiped out too much of old Helena.

Click. St. Helena Cathedral, modeled after the Vienna

The turn-of-the-century look of the Last Chance Gulch pedestrian mall downtown adds to Helena's charm. GARRY WUNDERWALD

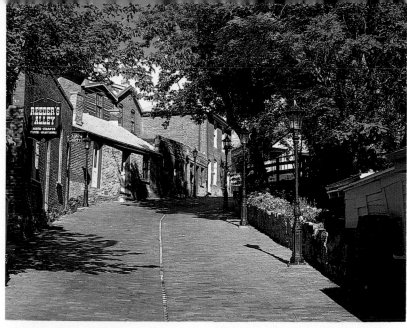

Once home to miners, Reeder's Alley now houses small shops and a fine restaurant. RICK GRAETZ

struction. The Shriners, however, had a difficult time maintaining the Moorish structure and the city took possession in 1935. As the Civic Center, it now is home to the Helena fire department and its auditorium and ballroom host many of Helena's cultural events. The Helena Symphony Orchestra, the Community Concert Series and the Helena Series for the Performing Arts all can be enjoyed here.

Click. Reeder's Alley, a miner's hostelry built in 1882 by Louis Reeder, is perhaps the best preserved block of property that has roots in Helena's mining era. Located at the foot of the alley is Pioneer Cabin, which was built in 1864. Reeder's Alley, like Pioneer Cabin, has managed to survive fire, flood, earthquake and Urban Renewal. Made of bricks shipped from St. Louis via steamboat, the alley marks the end of the old Benton Road stage line. Its interesting shops and the Stonehouse Restaurant belie its early reputation as the toughest section of town.

Right: *The Original Governor's Mansion on the corner of Sixth and Ewing, restored to 1890s style, is open for guided tours.*
Far right: *The minaret of the Helena Civic Center—originally built as a Shriner lodge—is a distinctive Helena landmark.*
RICK GRAETZ PHOTOS

Click. The Original Governor's Mansion, designed by architect Edgar Hodgson—who also designed the Lewis and Clark County Court House and Hauser's First National Bank—was built in 1888 as the family home of entrepreneur William Chessman, who would lose his fortune—and the house—in the Panic of 1893. After the turn of the century the Chessman mansion was home to Peter Larson, another entrepreneur who made his fortune in developing Montana. The state acquired the mansion in 1913 as the state's official governor's residence.

The mansion, now fully restored, sits on the corner of Ewing Street and Sixth Avenue. Nine Montana governors lived in the Victorian mansion during their terms. The mansion is administered by the Montana Historical Society and open for public viewing through guided tours most of the year.

Click. The Montana State Capitol is a fortress of Montana sandstone and granite

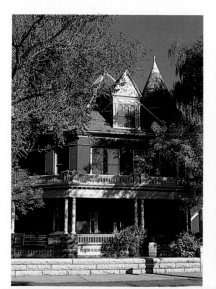

that serves as the working center of Montana democracy. It is a monument to Montana and the ferocious battles for the capital that Helena fought, over and over, since the 1860s. The Capitol, completed in 1902, houses Montana's executive and legislative branches of government. Paintings by Charles M. Russell and Edward Paxson adorn the walls and nobly document the early frontier. (History buffs and western-art connoisseurs might also visit the Montana Historical Society Museum and Library, located just across the street from the Capitol.)

The Capitol is a reflection of Greek neoclassical architecture and is listed on the National Register of Historic Places. Above all, the imposing strength of the structure seems to once and for all establish Helena as the center of Montana. Reminding us of the metal's importance to our history, copper covers the dome's exterior. A statue of the 1860s hero, the controversial Irish patriot and two-time acting territorial governor, Thomas Meagher, graces the Capitol garden.

Click. Carroll College, Montana's largest independent college, was founded in 1909 by Bishop John P. Carroll, then the Bishop of the Roman Catholic Diocese of Helena. Situated on 63 acres, the picturesque campus dominates the hill in north-central Helena. Carroll, long renowned for its pre-med pro-

The suitably flamboyant equistrian statue before the Montana Capitol is of Thomas Francis Meagher, Irish patriot who was twice acting governor of Montana Territory. The statue was a gift of Montana's Irish Americans.
TOM CORDINGLEY

gram, recently has established one of the premier forensic programs in the country and continues to support championship athletic programs.

Click. East Helena, established in 1888, is the area's factory town. The town's economy still is largely dependent on the Asarco lead smelter, one of only five in the world capable of processing lead or silver ores.

Click. Frontier Town, atop the Continental Divide on MacDonald Pass, is a favorite destination for cross-country skiers in winter and tourists looking for a real western fix and a hearty meal in summer. Some 15 years in the making, Frontier Town was a dream come true for the late John Quigley, who built this log and boulder Old West fort by hand.

Frontier Town atop MacDonald Pass. Weddings in the log chapel, steaks in the dining room, and drinks at the bar where "stools" are saddles attract Helenans and visitors. RICK GRAETZ

15

3 GOLD CAMP

As the story goes, by the summer of 1863 word from Montana had it that Alder Gulch was bearing chunks of gold that could be plucked from the ground by any cotton-picker. Easier pickings than California once offered. In 1863 what lured people west, away from the republic to an unknown wilderness, was certainly the power of gold. But these were radical, turbulent times with the country at war with itself, and the expanding territories also offered a place to run to, a chance to make a life, as opposed to simply living one.

Some seekers organized incredible caravans, and others trekked across the plains alone, leaving their war-torn homeland behind. Many came to find their fortune, many just came.

Every steamboat from St. Louis, Missouri to Fort Benton, Montana was said to be "weighed to the waterline" as it pushed up the Missouri River "with its cargo of human freight and supplies for the mine." All were bound for Virginia City, a crowded compound thick with thieves, killers and honorable men—but there was no telling one from the other.

Among the throng were John Cowan, John Crabb, D.J. Miller and Reginald "Bob" Stanley, typical frontier miners, who would be remembered in Helena as the "Four Georgians." Crabb came from Iowa. D.J. Miller hailed from Alabama, Reginald "Bob" Stanley from England, and only John Cowan, the last of the "Four

Top: Todd and Kara Graetz at the Pioneer Cabin on Park Avenue, one stop for the "Last Chancer" tour train, the popular summertime guided ride among historical sites. RICK GRAETZ
Bottom: Bird's-eye lithograph of Helena, 1865.
MONTANA HISTORICAL SOCIETY

Georgians," actually came from Georgia.

The frontier miners were caught, with hundreds of other fortune seekers, in the Virginia City/Alder/Bannack sluices, with little or nothing to do. Alder and Bannack gulches already were claimed and were being mined. There were probably as many men in the saloons looking for a claim to jump as there were men working claims in the hills. With gold fever high the best way to lower the population of the camps was to get the word out that "good colors"— that is

"gold"—had been found in a remote gulch. If one could be trusted, and if he wanted to rid the town of idle miners just before the good spring run-off, he might start a rumor while visiting Alder that some hard-luck tramps had struck it rich up Kootenai way, nearly 400 miles north through treacherous mountain country laced with suspicious Indian tribes growing less patient by the day with this second migration of persistent white men.

It seems that was how the eventual Four Georgians were ushered into the Kootenai

stampede. Stanley and Crabb, however, were more in the stampede's draft than its center. They had no luck in Virginia City but possibly were reluctant to leave because it would take weeks to reach the Kootenai and any day a nearby strike might be found. But, dejected, Crabb and Stanley eventually packed their animals and departed Virginia City for the rumor of gold in Kootenai country.

On their way north, while camped in the valley along the Clark Fork River, Crabb and Stanley met a mining party,

Above: *The Prickly Pear Valley (called Helena Valley locally) looking east from MacDonald Pass.* RICK GRAETZ

apparently led by James Coleman, that was returning from the Kootenai. There was no shout of "Eureka!" there. Coleman said the diggings were puny.

That night—it was in May, clear and cold—the word of the failed Kootenai expedition sailed through Hellgate like the haunting cry of a great horned owl. It reached another party of four miners late to leave Virginia City. Among that party were Georgian John Cowan and his Alabama soulmate, D.J. Miller, who had returned from prospecting

played-out California gold-rush haunts.

These were no hospitable digs. They had only a string of pack animals, beans, bacon, coffee and some tools to comfort their night. Once they realized they were aced out of Virginia City on a cold rumor, when the late-to-leave prospectors met and pitched stones into the campfire, they all must have felt a bit foolish. Maybe it was the Confederates, Cowan and Miller, who decided to strike out alone the next day. With the war still raging, there was little for

them to go home to. And they had Stanley's story of small riches scraped from the streams that fed the Blackfoot River to spur them on, in spite of the others who said they knew better than to believe the tall tales of the Englishman.

Still, it took several days for the disappointment of the Kootenai bust to subside. As prospectors headed back to Virginia City or other "secret" gulches, it was Cowan, Crabb, Stanley and Miller, probably about June 1, who become unlikely partners and decided

together to pan the Blackfoot River drainages.

Without the benefit of trails or compass, and with a waning faith in the ease of gold discovery, the four men followed the river to Nevada Creek and kept heading south and east over uncharted wilderness. Eventually, they reached the Continental Divide, south of the four-year-old Mullan Road. The cold spring rains and low fog made the wilderness trek a physical terror but when they dropped down the east slope of the Rockies and followed Ten Mile Creek to the Prickly Pear Valley, the elements didn't appear as formidable.

Left: Mullan Pass on the Continental Divide west of Helena was named for Lt. John R. Mullan, who built (1858-60) the military road that crossed here en route between Walla Walla, Washington Territory and Fort Benton and was popularly called the Mullan Road. GARRY WUNDERWALD

Some 19 years later, Stanley recalled the climb down the mountain to the great basin that the powerful Piegan Indians had long considered their "tona," or game pocket. He said the miner's "gladdened eyes swept the wide expanse of beautiful plains with its threading streams fringed with green-boughed cottonwoods. Bunch grass, fresh and luxuriant, waved everywhere, and herds of antelope, in scores and hundreds, fed unmolested—those nearest turning about and facing the party, wondering what intrusion of man upon their long unmolested preserves meant."

Time would tell. But as inviting as the valley appeared, after a night's camp and a small bit of prospecting in the gulch between Mount Ascension and Mount Helena the prospectors decided to leave the valley and continue north to prospect the maze of drainages that cut the Dearborn, Sun, Teton and Marias rivers. A more grueling, punishing horseback expedition in the rainy season is hard to imagine. To have reached the source of the Teton and the Marias rivers near the beginning of July, a swift journey to be sure, they could not have been doing much earnest

19

The partial ghost town of Rimini, west of Helena, served as a World War II training camp for sled-dog teams and mushers whose assignments included rescuing downed flyers in the Arctic.
GARRY WUNDERWALD

prospecting. It must have seemed all for naught.

In Montana Territory in 1864 everything was a gamble and time was the fortune seeker's currency. In this country, you can feel winter coming on even in the sweltering heat of July, and winter and defeat had to be on the prospectors' minds when they sat on the bank of the Marias River and decided to head back to the Prickly Pear Valley. If they didn't find gold, they would at least find some solace in the beauty of the valley before finally admitting failure. The prospecting was dim, the men desperate and they had begun to call that gulch in the Prickly Pear Valley their "last chance."

As Cowan, Crabb, Stanley and Miller approached the Prickly Pear Valley, the Union army crept toward Atlanta and a major, if not deciding, battle of the Civil War.

On the afternoon of July 14, 1864, as Gen. Sherman rebuilt the Chattahoochee River bridges to Atlanta that the Confederates had burned behind them, the prospectors crossed the Prickly Pear flats and wearily made their way up the gulch where they had camped six weeks earlier. "It's our last chance," one of the men said again.

They made camp farther up the gulch this time and fixed a supper. Some accounts put them on the intersection of Sixth and North Park, where the City/County Building sits. Other accounts place them at Sixth and Fuller, near the Montana Club.

Nevertheless, with the benefit of gracious light from Montana's long Arctic summer days, they moved out that evening to prospect. Cowan, Crabb and Miller dug in the lower reaches while Stanley went as far as a half-mile up the gulch to dig. There is some evidence that Crabb, the Yankee, didn't sympathize with his partners' Confederate politics. It's possible that Crabb chose to follow Cowan and Miller out of distrust.

So Stanley, alone, dug seven feet to bedrock. He panned the gravel from the bedrock in the small trickle of stream and saw about four flat nuggets. He plucked a nugget from the pan, held it up in the twilight and let it fall back into the pan. It had the sound of good weight and the ring of pure luck.

Stanley called for his partners and the four dug—near the Colwell Building on today's Last Chance Gulch mall—into the night. Satisfied that there was gold in the gulch they went back to camp. The howl of wolves and coyotes seemed to surround them and after firing rifle volleys into the pack to quiet the howls, the men agreed the camp would be called "Last Chance." In the

Facing page: The private Montana Club commissioned this Cass Gilbert–designed building to replace its original home on the same spot, built in 1893 and destroyed by fire in 1903.
RICK GRAETZ

Today's bullwhacker statue on the Last Chance Gulch pedestrian mall memorializes what once was a common sight, when ox teams from the river terminal of Fort Benton were this mining camp's lifeline. DARLENE DURGAN

following days, Stanley later said, "we set to and dug holes...took our time and did it well and chose what we thought was the best ground."

In the meantime, the prospectors officially laid plans for the camp and the law of the land. Last Chance would be in the Rattle Snake District which extended "three miles down, and up to the mouth of the canyon, and across from summit to summit."

They also set out to define the mining claims that would extend 200 feet up and down the gulch. Many of the long, narrow buildings on Last Chance Gulch today sit atop those defined claims. They called themselves "The Discovery Party" and gave themselves first rights to the meager water supply, the best claims and limited future

prospectors to two mining claims. They had been around long enough and had dreamed of a find for months. They knew exactly how to establish a camp before a stampede.

With that official work done and with their provisions running short, the Discovery Party chose Crabb and Cowan—a Yankee and a Confederate—to set out for Alder Gulch for supplies and a whipsaw to cut sluice boxes.

In a fortnight, Cowan and Crabb were back in Last Chance, and in Virginia City the *Montana Post* mentioned the strike in the same edition

that announced the success of Gen. Sherman's campaign on Atlanta. Dejected southern loyalists latched onto a rumor. In no time, word spread that four Georgians, Confederates, had struck it rich in a remote gulch to the north.

Judge Lyman E. Munson made his way to Helena in 1865 via the Missouri River. He arrived on a Sunday and he saw the town, built at the mouth of Last Chance Gulch where the Tertiary gravels were bearing gold in nuggets and dust. More than 100 houses were already built and 100 more were under construction. Rent was $200 a month, lodging hard to come by and wages terribly low. Already, speculators were buying and selling claims for small fortunes.

"This was a lively camp," the judge wrote in *Pioneer Life in Montana.* "Three thousand people were there, street spaces were blockaded with men and merchandise, ox trains, mule trains and pack trains surrounded the camp, waiting a chance to unload. The saw and hammer were

Marysville, northwest of Helena, today part ghost town, was the bustling community whose wealth included Thomas Cruse's fabulous Drumlummon Mine. JOHN REDDY

busy in putting up storehouses and in constructing sluice boxes for the washing out of gold, which was found in nearly every rod of its valley soil. Men, who had shunned domestic duty over the cradle for years, were rocking a cradle filled with dirty water, watching for appearances of golden sand to open their purse strings to the realities of their adventure.

"Auctioneers were crying their wares, trade was lively— saloons crowded—hurdy-gurdy dance houses were in full blast—wild mustang horses, never before saddled or bridled, with Mexican riders on their backs, where no man ever sat before, were running, jumping and kicking and bucking to unhorse their riders, much to the amusement of the jeering crowd, and as exciting as a Spanish bull fight."

On a hunch, on a cold, snowbound Sunday in March, I called Bud Guthrie's Prospector's Shop where a would-be prospector can purchase a plastic sluice pan or order a seriously deep bucket for a front-end loader. I asked Guthrie how his business was holding up. "Good," he said. I asked him to define "good," which he most agreeably did.

"Bud," I said, "what I really want to know is are folks still coming to town with the notion of striking it rich in gold."

Guthrie didn't miss a beat. "Oh, absolutely," he said. "Absolutely."

Bannack, Alder Gulch, Confederate Gulch, Last Chance Gulch, Park Gulch, Oro Fino Gulch, French Bar, Skelly Gulch, Greenhorn

Mid Canon, Missouri Riv.

Gulch, Dry Gulch, the Scratch-gravel Hills, Grizzly Gulch, Unionville, *et al.,* owe their gold and memories to the Boulder Batholith. Their placers all were laced with the gold washed from the batholith's eroded mother lodes.

In events that occurred about 200 million years ago, the continental plate crashed, the west coast crumpled like a subcompact, the earth's crust heated up tremendously. About 78 million years ago, out of the blue the Elkhorns started spewing molten rock. Then an asteroid the size of Chicago beaned the earth, throwing evolution for a loop and all the while pieces of water-borne gold were dumped into cracks of the batholith's cooling rock. Along comes a creature with no million-year

credentials who has a hankering for gold just when erosion has the batholith brushing ore off its balding head like dandruff. That is the sheerest, blindest luck.

There is batholith-generated gold still to be found planted in the hills, no doubt. Montana Tunnels, a modern multimillion-dollar gold and silver mining operation 25 miles south of Helena, is sifting the dirt in a gigantic hole known as a diatreme. The gargantuan mine is in the middle of a historic gold and silver mining district—Wicks, Corbin, Alta—transformed by the Boulder Batholith. The Montana Tunnels diatreme is laced with minute amounts of gold and silver ore hidden within the tons of volcanic debris caused in part by the batholith. An-

other industrial-sized gold mine is being planned near Winston.

But as John McPhee points out in his wonderful book *Basin and Range,* "gold is not merely rare. It can be said to love itself." By resisting a union with other elements it has acquired both its value and its timeless nobility.

Helena's bedrock lodes of gold were formed after the batholith assaulted the earth's crust, but before the volcanoes died. Hot springs, fueled by the magma, were fiercely active. Many still dot the region and many geologists believe the batholith is still harboring deep magmatic activity.

Like a pirate's "X" marking the spot of buried treasure, hot springs can pinpoint sources of vein ore deposits. Col. Broadwater's hot springs west of Helena and the Boulder Hot Springs are two of the area's more famous ones, but the entire region is pocked with active and inactive hot springs.

The hot water circulating deep within the earth picks up its freight of elements and minerals being forced from the

Streetcars ran from town to the hot-springs spa (hotel, left; natatorium, right) built by Charles A. Broadwater west of Helena. MONTANA HISTORICAL SOCIETY

subterranean pressure cooker. The hot water continues to add to its cargo as it rises. The minerals are transported in solution and carried through a tortuous course of rock. Upon reaching surface-cool rock, the water temperature drops. The cooling water cannot keep the heavy gold in solution, and it is dumped along the course. Motherlodes—from Old English "lad," way or course—are fissures in hard crustal rock where the cooling water's mineral freight was dumped.

Water dumps silicon from solution at nearly the same temperature as it dumps gold. It is rare, however, when they are dumped together. But when silicon is unloaded with gold, it clings to it and weaves its rockmate a quartz cocoon.

Helena miners did love quartz, but they learned to despise it too, because they expected too much of it. Many figured that gold was to be found in every quartz vein. One only had to dig deeper to find the ore. That backward notion tore the heart out of Helena's gold industry in the 1880s. Deep was not the an-

Rugged passage in Wolf Creek Canyon, north of town, about 1885. COURTESY JEAN BAUCUS

25

swer. There is no method of finding gold in quartz. None exists. No secrets, just lucky strikes and few of them.

Last Chance, a placer strike, is thought to have produced $170,000 in gold its first year and $10 to $35 million before it played out. Alta, near Corbin, offered up $32 million between 1883 and 1910. The Whitlatch-Union Mine in Unionville produced $6 million in gold over 40 years. Tommy Cruse's Drumlummon Mine in Marysville, the product of a smaller magmatic intrusion, made Cruse's fortune.

When the building boom struck Helena in the late 1880s the Helena newspapers regularly ran short news items on the discovery of gold nuggets during excavation work. In 1917, after a spring deluge, a bank president found "a gold nugget as big as a marble" in front of the Placer Hotel, the building that now houses the Overland Express Restaurant. The find prompted what the papers called "a placer mining bonanza" along the curbs, streets and gutters of Helena. In 1948, gold was found by workmen digging a new elevator shaft for the Placer Hotel. But by then, with only $1.75 in paying dust in every cubic yard of dirt, gold must have lost some of its attraction. "We don't have time to

Above: Time out to pose for the camera at the Legal Tender Mine in the Clancy area, date unknown.
MONTANA HISTORICAL SOCIETY

Mountain biking on the divide between Oro Fino and Dry gulches south of Helena. Mt. Helena city park includes the land in the background. RICK GRAETZ

mess with gold," was the final word from a hotel official.

During the 1970s urban renewal spree, excavated downtown building sites were successfully sluiced for gold. In the spring of 1985, after a deluge washed tons of eroded soil from the gulches, a friend who lives on Davis Street, on the lower reaches of Dry Gulch, sifted the flood sediments in his basement and found paying quantities of gold dust.

On August 27, 1864, the first edition of Montana's first newspaper, the *Montana Post,* carried news of the Four Georgians' strike. "On Dry Creek, between Silver Creek and Prickly Pear, gold has been recently discovered, and a big stampede has taken place there. The scarcity and distance that water has to be brought will make it expensive and though the ground may pay, enough is not known to create a stampede. Usually at those points parties interested get up sensation rumors to get a rush. The boys should be on their guard."

I have begun to believe that even then, a month after the discovery, the location of the strike, more than the strike itself, made the businessmen of Virginia City tremble. More people were coming to the territory by the day. Last Chance had better access to Fort Benton, Silver City, Gold Creek, Hellgate and Montana City. The geography made it a natural. Smarter and better financed men were looking for ways for Montana to produce for the States. Gold could facilitate financial backing but it could not be depended on to make a state economy. California and Colorado had proved that beyond a doubt. One needed agriculture, skilled laborers, merchants and ease of transportation to keep a western city of the 1860s alive for maps yet to be printed in the 1880s. The Prickly Pear Valley offered it all.

Montana City area in northern Jefferson County, where the rural lifestyle has attracted commuters employed in Helena. RICK GRAETZ

4 NAMING HELENA

T*he Helena Herald now, for the second or third time, prints the record of the proceeding at a meeting held in Last Chance, which ought to effectively settle the matter.*"

Helena Herald,
February 13, 1892

The matter of how Helena received its name was no less effectively settled then than it is now, but it is certain that by the fall of 1864 there were some who showed up in camp itching to sell the first silk hats to dusty-capped prospectors and the name "Last Chance City" just wouldn't do.

Some accounts insist that Helena was named after a miner's Minnesota sweetheart. Another says it was originally "St. Helena," after the island where Napoleon was exiled. A California man wrote to the Montana Historical Society in 1962 with the notion that the town was named for his grandmother.

But the dynamics of early-day Helena suggest a finer calculation.

Once it became clear where Last Chance was situated— just a few miles from the Old North Trail used by all of the Northern Plains Indians to reach the buffalo country— those in the Territory with political and entrepreneurial aspirations saw Last Chance as a buried commercial and merchandising treasure waiting to be unearthed.

The geography naturally offered north-to-south transit via the Missouri River and the historical east-to-west transit through the Rocky Mountains, made somewhat more

By September 1864 there were five cabins in Helena. Bob Stanley and John Cowan built the first two cabins. Other cabins were built by members of a small party, less led than persuaded to the camp by the politically ambitious Captain George J. Wood from Illinois.

The camp wasn't yet eight weeks old, but hundreds of prospectors already had staked empty claims in Last Chance and soon left for better diggings. Still, on October 1, 1864, 200 men were in Last Chance to choose their representatives for the Montana Territorial Legislature.

After the vote, a growing segment of the camp did not relish the idea of wintering in a place called "Last Chance." It was simply too crass.

It is a sure bet that would-be merchants and political hopefuls could not live with the deadly ring of "Last Chance" when the territory's leading town had a more alluring name in Virginia City.

On October 30, 1864, a group of at least seven men—some accounts maintain there were

inviting by the well-known Mullan Road, must have raised some speculative eyebrows. Chances are, an agricultural distribution town would eventually have been established here or near here. But the logical geographic beauty of its location combined with the discovery of gold to hasten and heighten political and commercial development.

The mansion district of Helena's upper west side was a mixture of urban and rural when this turn-of-the-century photo was taken.
COURTESY JEAN BAUCUS

as many as 40 but considering the design of the tiny, low-ceilinged cabins, that is unlikely—met in Capt. Wood's cabin. Wood had been stumping for the meeting for some time and made no secret that he was seeking a political position for himself and for his father-in-law.

Also among the men was Cornelius Hedges, a Yale and Harvard graduate who later served Montana as U.S. Attorney, Superintendent of Public Instruction, Probate Judge, Historical Society secretary and a loan association president. Clearly, even at this early date, not everyone in Last Chance was interested in dirtying his hands with placer mining.

The meeting was called to name the town, elect commissioners and authorize the design and layout of the streets. The latter two items on the agenda were handled easily, the naming was another matter.

Many accounts indicate that the gentlemen were discussing the merits of calling the town "Tomah," in honor of an Indian chief who frequented the camp or as a shortened version of "tomahawk." The name under discussion was more likely "Tonah," a phonetic spelling of the Blackfeet word for their Helena area hunting grounds: "tona," which meant "game pocket."

Being the day before Halloween, some of the less ambitious gentlemen at the meeting offered "Pumpkinville" and "Squashtown" as proper names for the camp. "Winona" and "Rochester," after Minnesota

This fountain in Hill Park, at the north end of the downtown business district, was dedicated by the Daughters of the Confederacy in 1916. Many of Montana Territory's original settlers had fled the War Between the States—from both sides of the Mason-Dixon line. JOHN REDDY

towns, also were offered.

Tonah, however, was getting the most reluctant support until John Summerville, described as a tall, angular, frank, intelligent and grizzled Scotsman, rose from his pine block and proposed to call the camp "HeLEENa."

The men in the room grumbled. When Summerville spelled the name—h-e-l-e-n-a—the Confederate loyalists could hardly be controlled. The southerners pronounced the word HELena, as they did in Helena, Arkansas, the location of a strategic port on the Mississippi River.

"Do you propose this place in honor of that rebel city in Arkansas?" T.E. Cooper, the secretary of the meeting, shouted above the rebel yells.

Summerville, whom most everyone called Uncle John because of his years and his friendly manner, did not take kindly to the Confederate association. "Not by a damned sight, sir," the old man boomed. When the room quieted he continued: "I propose to call it HeLEENa, in honor of the HeLEENa in Scott County, Minnesota, the best county in the state and the best state in the Union, by God."

And HeLEENa she became and stayed until 1882 and the arrival of the Northern Pacific Railroad. At that point, and no one is quite sure why, the people here began to accent the word on the first syllable and the pronunciation became the softer and more genteel: *Helen*-a.

In 1906, "Georgian" Bob Stanley, who was at that October 30, 1864 meeting, wrote that he "was surprised to find the accent changed to Helena when it was christened and pronounced Heleena." It might comfort Stanley to know that town we call *Hel*ena will probably always be known as HeLEENa to much of the rest of the nation.

Facing page: Successful hunting on the Hilger ranch north of Helena in the 1890s.
MONTANA HISTORICAL SOCIETY

5 WEALTH

At a party I let it be known that I believed nearly $3 million was dropped in Helena for its major building projects in 1888.

No one blinked an eye.

The Novelty Block at $20,000. The Atlas Block at $40,000. The Pittsburgh Block at $40,000. The Granite Block at $15,000. The Gold Block at $40,000. The Iron Front at $50,000. The Steamboat Block at $35,000. The Broadwater Hotel at $125,000. Some 400 new residences at $800,000 and 14 mansions at $136,000. The streetcar system was extended and a new steam motor line was added. Sewer lines and streets were being built.

The *Helena Record,* on January 1, 1889, ran this headline: "How a City Is Made in One Year." The reporter wrote:

Top: The Pittsburgh Block, seen here not long before urban renewal projects transformed the downtown in the 1970s, was among the many business blocks built in 1888. COURTESY JEAN BAUCUS
Below: *A.C. Johnson, banker and insurance-company founder, built this home in 1894.* RICK GRAETZ

"Architects from the largest cities in the land, who had been located here for some time engaged principally in building structures of a modest nature, now began to adorn the walls of their offices with plans of impossible fairy-like structures which the average spectator was prone to call offspring of a diseased mental condition."

I was becoming convinced that the people with money must have believed they were given it to burn. The reaction among my friends at the party, who were mostly my age, was unanimous. "Big deal."

At another party I was collared by an elderly woman. She kept repeating to me her childhood vision of the handsome Helena millionaire driving around town on summer Sundays with his family. She could still describe the red open-air, self-propelled coach, the millionaire and the vicarious pride her mother and father took in seeing the well heeled family on its Sunday tool about town.

My reaction? Big deal.

Weeks later it struck me that my reaction, if not purely cynical, was at least typical of people in Helena of my age who are confronted almost daily with "the rich history." To us, the names Power, Hauser, Holter, Broadwater, Cruse and Davis are Helena streets and dams. But to the people a few generations removed, they are the names of kings and Helena is the kingdom they forged from the wilderness.

Back to the *Helena Record,* January 1, 1889: "Already people who wandered inquiringly among piles of brick and mortar began to see that a city was in the course of construc-tion, not a place for the storage of goods, buying and selling, and the transactions of such a business as might come along, but a modern city with all that term implies, a place to live in,

to settle down in, in calm contentment and with a feeling of equality with the rest of the world."

Surely the reporter suffered from the journalistic hubris that defines the age but certainly Helena had found the money to somehow buy what every frontier town wanted—equality with the rest of the world, especially the world east of the Mississippi River.

Within a single generation, some 20 years after the discovery of gold, Helena became the leading financial and industrial center of the region. The question is always, why Helena? Historical researchers say convincingly that unlike the Leadvilles, the Bannacks, and the Nevada Citys of the frontier, Helena quickly assumed an aura of community because, of all things, the geography.

Helena became a redistribution point for freight unloaded at the Fort Benton levee for delivery at Montana's gold camps. Because Helena sat at the crossroads of the main east-to-west and north-to-south wagon roads, the multiplying post-Civil War merchants set up shop in Helena and grew with the territory.

It has been suggested that the initial mining push was composed less of a mix of prospectors and farmers than land speculators constantly seeking the end of the rainbow. Joseph Kinsey Howard, in his astute book *Montana: High,*

Wide and Handsome, writes that "Montana was a no-man's land, to be looted by the strongest and, as soon as possible, abandoned. One owed it no allegiance."

The miners often made their pile and split for the states. Yet, for the merchants and businessmen, Helena actually sat at the end of the rainbow for nearly 30 years. When the placers were played out, the rich quartz lodes were mined with industrial investments from abroad. Large mining companies made their corporate headquarters in Helena and the labor force settled in. Many of the original Helena businessmen—and there were some 180 businesses and six banks in Helena by 1867—socked their extra money into expansion, the business blocks downtown and mining and real estate investments.

The Homer building once stood at the corner of Park and Clarke.
COURTESY JEAN BAUCUS

Farmers and ranchers located in the valley to supply the village with food. By 1874 Helena's community influence brought the territorial capital to town and, despite several vicious battles to have it moved, the political center of Montana has managed to remain in Helena.

In the 1880s there were six national banks in Helena and 22 trains veered in and out of town daily, giving residents better access to other states than we have today.

Big deal? Actually, in comparison to the ventures of Eastern capitalists—J.P. Morgan, Andrew Carnegie, John D. Rockefeller—no, it wasn't a very big deal. And Hauser and Cruse and Power and Holter and Broadwater are not names you will find in grander sweeps of American history or even surveys of the great industrial era of American capitalism. They were really like many of us here today. Here because they could accomplish some things in a lifetime without getting lost in the shuffle, yet, when you walk down Last Chance Gulch, tour the west side and the wild architecture of the Victorian-era mansions, it is painfully evident that they pined for that kind of recognition and power and they were optimistic enough to believe that it would come to them.

At least that is what their lavish spending and building and booming led everyone to believe. That's what the elderly woman at the party believed as she told me over and over again about the millionaire's Sunday drive around town. "Oh, in that red coach on a Sunday after church, it was a sight to behold."

I have to believe that it was indeed.

Mt. Helena rises above the upper west side. RICK GRAETZ

35

6 HANGMAN'S TREE

I walked from my house to Dry Gulch—Davis Street, now—and tried to have the gulch tell me where the roots of Hangman's Tree would lead. The tree from which at least 10 men "were hanged from the neck until dead" once stood in Dry Gulch, near the corner of Blake and Hillsdale streets.

I was haunted by a dead man's reminiscence. He was H. Frank Adkins and he had arrived in Helena with his parents, Main Street merchants they were, in 1865. H. Frank Adkins died here 47 years later. That's not so long ago.

Adkins told a man once that he could still "recall that one morning, as I was putting some of the goods out for a display, a German who had a place next to ours said, 'I see that the old pine tree stills bears fruit'."

The teen-aged Adkins smiled and nodded his head, but didn't get it. "This was something I didn't understand," he later admitted, "but I would not let on that I did not know."

Among H. Frank Adkins's chores on June 6, 1866 was gathering wood. As usual he walked past the jail. That morning, however, the door was wide open and the room vacant. Blood was on the floor. Adkins turned on his heels but the German merchant was busily talking to a pedestrian.

There was talk in the camp. Dry Gulch.

"I went up Dry Gulch and saw the old pine with its 'fruit'," Adkins continued. "This time in the shape of Frenchy."

Frenchy, whose Christian name was John Crochet, had been a night watchman on Last Chance Gulch. He was hanged by the neck and dead. The Vigilantes had marked the body "3-7-77," the never-explained inscription left on all their Alder Gulch victims, which is part of the Montana Highway Patrol's insignia to this day.

Anyway, the Vigilantes also posted the body, as was their

Fifty years after Vigilante activity, Helena wore a civilized face for this Fourth of July, 1910 scene. Compare the original streetlamps along Main Street to their modern replacements (page 12).
COURTESY JEAN BAUCUS

custom, with the unlawfully executed man's offense.

"This man, Frenchy, was hanged for stealing $700 from an old grey headed man and also for trying to swear away the lives of innocent men."

An unofficial account contends that Frenchy rolled a drunk old man for $700 in gold dust. He spent $400 of the loot that night, picking up tabs and playing the big shot. Frenchy,

Top: *Skihi Peak, Helena National Forest, seen from the divide between Davis and Oro Fino gulches.* RICK GRAETZ
Right: *Employees of an early-day bordello.* COURTESY JEAN BAUCUS

showing some remorse, returned to the beaten old man the remaining $300. By June 5, Frenchy was officially fingered and that night he was hanged. Just two months earlier, the Vigilantes had strung up James Daniels from the very same Hangman's Tree.

Daniels was a gambling tough accused of murder and convicted of manslaughter. Acting Territorial Governor Thomas Francis Meagher pardoned Daniels. When he was released from jail, Daniels wandered about Helena to even the score against the men who "sent him up." The Vigilantes wasted no time. Daniels was lynched on Hangman's Tree and pinned to the corpse was a note for Acting Governor Meagher: "Do this again and you'll meet the same fate."

On July 1, 1866 Meagher allegedly fell off a riverboat en route to Fort Benton and drowned in a shallow stretch of the Missouri River. His body was never found and rumors persist that Vigilantes had condemned and executed Thomas Meagher.

I thought about the sound of those two syllables, "Dry Gulch," as I walked through the neighborhoods. I wondered what chords they struck on Main Street, circa 1866. Dry Gulch. It was remote from Helena. But by the 1880s it

would be the middle of the residential area. Once a good place to hang a man at night, back in the hills, away from town, Dry Gulch would become a good place to live.

Up the gulch, the signs of placer diggings are still evident. It is still dirt road and the gravels are still in piles. Imagining the workings, the era suddenly seems lonely and desperate.

Walking the neighborhoods the whole idea of vigilance committees loses its romance, too. I find it to be the remnants of venomous hype for post-Civil War Eastern newspaper readers whose vision of the frontier was clouded by the smoke of industrialization and prosperity. I think of the high school's "Vigilante Stadium" and the annual "Vigilante Day Pa-

In Colorado Gulch, west of Helena. RICK GRAETZ

rade," where high-school students portray many nonviolent themes from Montana history.

Walking, I thought these neighborhoods beautiful and quiet. I knew I could knock on virtually any door and be invited in. That is a characteristic of these old neighborhoods and the people who inhabit them. But I could well imagine the masked Vigilantes on dark horses, a team pulling a flatbed wagon up the hard-packed dirt to the Dry Gulch and Hangman's Tree.

The Vigilantes were the subject of the first book to be published in Montana—*The Vigilantes of Montana,* by Thomas J. Dimsdale. Mark Twain called it a "blood thirsty little book," and Charles Dickens was so taken with the enigmatic character of X. Biedler, the so-called "Vigilante executioner," that he expressed a desire to meet X. X. made his home in Helena. He is buried here.

In a letter home to Germany, Heinrich John Henry Jurgens commended the night-time hangings as good Western justice but lamented that in

Hail blankets Helena during a violent 1982 storm. Central School and St. Helena Cathedral are in right background. DARLENE DURGAN

daytime Helena, "No person knows how to recognize another and no one knows how to handle another." I thought about that social uncertainty as I approached Dry Gulch.

In 1876, the Reverend Mr. W.C. Shippen paid a man $2.50 to cut the tree down. "Well, when the news reached town almost a riot followed," Rev. Shippen told a Butte newsman years later. "Scores of people visited my place and in a short time they had taken away most of the tree as souvenirs. I did not know how much the people appreciated the gruesome old relic."

Mr. Shippen allegedly had canes made from the felled tree, but he would need more than that to help steady his mission. Within a short time, he was shipped to Butte and Helena's Methodist Episcopal Church had a new pastor.

Sometime later a fire engulfed the property and burned even the stump to ash. After the fire, X. Biedler himself, corpulent and ugly, came up Dry Gulch with a shovel and an ax intent on salvaging a piece of the tree for posterity.

From old photographs, even in the fading spring twilight I thought I could discern where Hangman's Tree had stood. I was struck by a revelation. The tree was always dead. No one in Helena had ever seen the tree alive.

It was soon dark and I could see the flame-like flicks of color television light bounce against drapes and windows of several homes. I wondered if they knew what happened here. I could knock and ask, but I thought better of it.

I sat on the curb and looked at the space where Hangman's Tree stood. James Daniels killed a man sitting across the table from him in a card game. Pulled out his gun and blew him away. Imagine the powerful recoil of his Colt pistol; imagine the heft of the gun, the sharp smell of gun powder and whiskey and the horror of the witnesses to the killing.

A trolley car heading up West Sixth Avenue on a snowy day reveals pollution problems of a bygone time.
MONTANA HISTORICAL SOCIETY

The modern gunplay in our valley has been met with horror and outrage, too. There is more gunplay in Chicago and Detroit, St. Louis and New York and Miami in one day than Helena has seen in two years, but our horror is magnified because that monster is not supposed to live here. I think we become unnerved.

We tend to check the door before bed and feel uncomfortable about having to do it. We tend to wonder, a mile away from home, if we locked the garage. It's an uneasy feeling because we are no longer convinced that Helena is just a sleepy little town.

When violence strikes and the newspaper graphically outlines the position of the dead with spread-eagled stick figures and the get-away with bold treasure-map dashes, people talk on the street. "They should string up the s.o.b." "Just put him out of his misery." I heard that, sitting there on the curb, looking for the tree and I said to myself, "X.? X., is that you?"

Above: *Le Grande Cannon Road (named for the son of a pioneer Helena merchant) halfway up Mt. Helena follows the pathway of sluices that brought water into the mining camp in the earliest days.*
LESTER LOBLE

41

7 WHAT IT IS: PENTURBIA

For all its beauty and history, there is a sense that Helena, post-1910, survived but did not progress. The events of the nation made history, but not the events of Helena, not like the old days.

Precious little has defined Helena since the gold rush and building boom. The depression, the World Wars, earthquakes. There is not much to separate Helena from other places.

But there might be now. A Washington State University professor has an interesting theory that appears to fit Helena and its current psyche. The professor, Jack Lessinger, believes he has mapped the latest major migration in America. He says people are turning to smaller towns and cities and away from the metropolitan areas that have been the focus of most of our lives throughout this century.

Lessinger, who published his theory in *American Demographics,* in 1987, says the shift represents a change in values as Americans move from consumerism to conservationism. He told the

With the influence of federal, state, county and city governments, Helena is a white-collar community. State government is the largest employer and the federal government the second largest. White-collar employment in Helena was 144 percent of the national average in the last census.

It is interesting to note that these caring conservers are demanding planned development to prevent runaway growth and that they feel older buildings are both rich in nostalgia and less expensive than new construction. All are issues that have been addressed, and often bitterly fought, in Helena over the past decade. Lessinger says the shift in values is most likely to emerge in places that grew rapidly in the nation's early history, hit a plateau at the turn of the century and then decelerated until 1970, with a particularly slow growth rate between 1950 and 1970. If that's the case, then Helena is a center of penturbia, and the shift, and the people who effect it, may make history here.

Associated Press that the shift is being manifested in small cities and towns where industrial and commercial districts are interspersed with farms, forests, rivers and lakes.

Lessinger says the shift is led by the "caring conserver," who saves and guards resources, works for preservation of air, water, buildings, parks and cultural artifacts.

Helena fits the profile and appears to the ideal "penturbia," a word Lessinger coined to depict the fifth major migration in the U.S. since the American Revolution. Consider (according to the 1980 census) that the population of Helena between 25 and 35 was 113 percent of the national average.

Helenans are highly educated. College graduates make up 26 percent of the population over 25 years old, 161 percent of the national average.

Facing page: Helena's Federal Building anchors the south end of downtown's mall. JOHN REDDY

8 HELENA TODAY

In round numbers there are about 24,000 people living in Helena and 13,000 more surrounding them, mostly in the Helena Valley, but there are folks in the hills—Unionville, for instance—and others on 20 acres apiece, much of that land vertical, in the gulches outside of town. The Chamber of Commerce likes to point out that Helena is in the center of a 250-mile bubble that covers more than 70 percent of the residents of Montana.

That imaginary enclosure does create an atmosphere that civically proud western towns have became good at—placing themselves smack in the middle of the action, real or imagined.

It has become something of a Western signature.

Nevertheless, the nearest mega-city to the west is Seattle, a 600-mile trek. Minneapolis lies more than 1,000 miles due east and Denver is a not-unpleasant 15-hour drive south. At this juncture one cannot purchase a direct-flight airline ticket to Seattle, Minneapolis or Denver for departure from the Helena Regional Airport. An inconvenience, sure, but consider

The copper-domed Montana Capitol. RICK GRAETZ

that Helena is one of the least populated state capitals in the nation. It has a smaller population than even Cheyenne, the capital of Wyoming, our least populated state. There was a period in the mid-1980s when Helena couldn't support a taxi service. With its one television station, Helena is the third-smallest network-affiliated TV market in the country—falling behind are only Selma, Alabama and Glendive.

Outside the gates of the city there are fewer people still, but life is teeming. Big-game species include elk, mule deer and white-tailed deer, bighorn sheep, black bears, antelopes, moose and mountain goats. Cottontail rabbits, snowshoe hares and upland birds, given the chance, abound. Mountain lions, lynxes, beavers, musk-rats, martens, fishers and river otters are common.

Bald eagles winter near Lake Helena, and in spring and summer ospreys claim the upper Missouri River. Balds in winter and ospreys in summer. That alone is enough to keep some people around for a good

long time. The rich land is shared by prairie falcons, red-tailed hawks, kestrels, sparrow hawks, great horned owls, and that big river invites white pelicans and herons to nest.

One of the largest waterfowl flyways in the state is located in the central portion of Lewis and Clark County. The county also contains world-class

grizzly bear habitat and that may be good or bad, depending on one's point of view. Three areas in the county are designated as "Class I—Highest Value Fishery" resources by federal and state agencies. They are the three, one- to five-mile stretches directly below Hauser, Holter and Canyon Ferry lakes on the Missouri River.

Facing page, top: Governor's Cup marathoners run from Marysville into Helena. RICK GRAETZ
Bottom: Montana Department of Justice building in the capitol complex. JOHN REDDY *Right: "It's always Friday in Montana," said a 1986 promotion. Here, on the Missouri River.* JOHN REDDY

Too, six sites near Helena have been considered for designation as national natural landmarks. They are Beartooth Game Range, tucked behind Holter Lake; the Gates of the Mountains Wilderness; Granite Butte near Stemple Pass; Green Timber Basin/Beaver Creek; Red Mountain and the Sun River Game Range. And, under consideration for wilderness designation is Black Mountain, just beyond Mount Helena. The area encompasses the Ten Mile Creek watershed and Blackhall Meadows—walking distance from the steps of the Capitol.

It's only a piece of Helena, Montana, this place once at the crossroads of the northern plains that was unfathomably wealthy and competitive. The merchants, manufacturers, miners and speculators who drove Helena years ago have been replaced by the wheels of government and the service

industries that support them—the schools, hospitals and telephone and power companies. It is an uncomplicated town even if three of Helena's top five major employers are government. Government is Helena's basic industry, its economic bedrock that accounts for nearly 70 percent of the hometown economic base. In addition to being the capital, and running its own incorporated city government, Helena is the federal government's headquarters in Montana and the county seat of Lewis and Clark County.

All of which has lent Helena the economic stability while its sister cities have been rocked, jostled and uplifted by the various economic factors—from the boardfoot price of timber and the per-barrel cost of oil, to the bucks offered for steers on the hoof, and malting barley—on which most other Montana communities rely.

That is not to say that life here is absolutely hunky-dory. This is a real place, full of real people with real ambitions, emotions, expectations.

Jim Hughes came to Helena from Colorado in 1971 with Mountain Bell and the first wave of sustained population growth Helena experienced in nearly two decades. He is a lobbyist for Mountain Bell who is not dyed in stiff conservative wool as one expects of executives. While being active in groups that attempt to find ways to lure new businesses—"economic development" has become the key phrase—to Montana, Hughes maintains an interest in community values and searches for developments that utilize, not exploit, Montana's resources. It is not an easy task, which reinforces Hughes' conviction that Helena's cool dependence on government

Jim Hughes, lobbyist for Mountain Bell. JOHN REDDY

jobs may be myopic and not in the town's best interests.

"The government jobs and the large business or two in town have created capabilities most towns the size of Helena don't have," Hughes says. "I don't know of a town this size that could possibly have the resources for a symphony orchestra or a theater that works year-round and makes a go of it. Helena has a unique mix and match of people, but at the same time, the whole plan to create an environment is lacking. I don't think there is something that says there's a vision for the future.

"I have been trying to talk to state legislators about that for Montana," Hughes continues. "Create a vision for people to buy into. Helena doesn't have a broad base. It's simply depending on [government] jobs and that dependence makes for a real critical atmosphere in the overall economy. It could be similar to an eastern industrial town after the steel mills shut down. We're all pointing to that stability, but is it really there?"

Interestingly, fewer than 100 years ago, Helena capitalist

posed of the husband-and-wife work team. The national average is about six percent. And, together, the Helena husband-and-wife team averages a $22,200 annual income.

If there is a moral to be found there, it is that you have to make some sacrifices to live in Helena, or most anywhere else in the northern Rockies, where the per-capita income in 1985 was $11,429, about $800 less than the per-capita income of the folks in Lewis and Clark County.

There is a notion that the real West is all landscape brimming with freedom and that money is a secondary consideration, tucked in the rumble seat of a prized social vehicle known as "quality of life." Sometimes, in Helena, the notion becomes comfortably trapped between the buildings on Last Chance Gulch. The landscape beyond—the "Class A" scenery along the Missouri River, in Wolf Creek Canyon, in the Gates of the Mountains Wilderness and along the unspeakably mysterious Rocky

and one-time governor of Montana Territory Samuel Hauser boasted that Helena had more millionaires per capita than any other city in the world. Four generations hence, Helena appears to possess more working couples, more two-income families, than most other American cities. About 20 percent of Helena's total population is com-

Mountain Front where the great bear walks—is but a convenient backdrop for the Western myth.

But backdrop or no, now and again, at 40 below zero on a thin white November day you can get close to the brittle isolation, and that notion of radical freedom is a lonely thing that forces you to think about your life here.

"Here is sanctity," Ralph Waldo Emerson wrote, "which shames our religions and reality which discredits our heroes. Here we find Nature to be the circumstance which dwarfs every other circumstance, and judges like a god all men that come to her."

The words may be Emerson's, but the emotions are periodically shared among most of the people who choose to live in Helena. Still, this is a city where landscape and isolation can transcend even the Transcendentalists. Helenans are an educated lot. More than 26 percent of the population over 25 years of age are college graduates. (The corresponding national average is 16 percent.) That makes for a lot of Philosophy, Psychology and Sociology 101 veterans cramped on the street reaching for theoretical cause and effect connections.

That is one reason why so much has been made about the idea that the people of Helena are somehow more aloof than their fellow Montanans.

Butte is a staunch blue-collar, shot-and-beer town. Missoula, even with its intellectual underground, is a timber–industry citadel. Billings is oil. Great Falls is Malmstrom Air Force Base and the Strategic Air Command. And nearly everywhere else is cattle and winter wheat. In that milieu, Helena is an easy mark: White-collar sophisticates. Bureaucrats.

Although it may seem a quaint country town to mega-city dwellers, to other Montanans Helena is Montana-urban sans cowboy. The town is a veritable white-collar cavalry. There are more than twice as many white-collar workers in Helena than the national average. And the city's occupations are different from those in other Montana cities and towns. Here it is office work that requires close and daily interaction among people who are usually highly specialized. In Helena, the people also have a wide variety of cultural expression—Grand Street community theater, the Helena Symphony, the annual traditional jazz festival, small college and high school ath-

letics, Minor League baseball, golf, softball, the Helena Series for the Performing Arts, Community Concerts, Second Story Cinema.

In the rural areas, where the lifestyle is tied more closely to the land and its seasonal rhythms, one's sense of isolation comes not from the landscape but from the growing white-collar populations. Traditional rural work demands a wider range of skills and more self-sufficiency than that in the city. Government is suspect just over the hill in Deep Creek Canyon, up Augusta way, or on the ranches outside Clancy where life is at a slower pace and where the people place more emphasis on traditional values.

"Obviously my concerns with Helena and the surrounding area are not economic," says Ralph Beer, who was born and raised south of Helena on his family's homestead ranch. Beer is a novelist—his first novel, *The Blind Corral,* was published by Viking Penguin in 1986 and won the 1986 Western Writers Book Award—and a teacher at Helena's Carroll College. However, he continues to run cows on the 1,000-acre ranch that now is surrounded by the modern West's version of Levittown—five- to 20-acre ranchettes. "This morning," Beer says, "I was in mud up to my knees trying to get a calf out of a cow. If you are still messing with cows [these days], you're essentially not interested in making money."

Although Beer's ranch is a quick 10 miles from the city limits, culturally and psychologically the ranch is a world apart. "It seems to me," Beer says, "when you talk about Helena, you're talking about two towns, two places. The wonderful place on the west side with all its neighborhoods around the cathedral, and then you're talking about the Helena Valley where I think there was more violence and gunplay in the past year [a reference to several shootings in 1986-87] than in the heyday of Dodge City. It seems to me, when a discrepancy like that happens in such tight quarters, it happens because people treat each other so differently. You can come uptown today and walk around and people are nice, but it may be a lot different in [some places in the valley]."

Beer has spoken often and eloquently about the sting that "discrepancy" has caused his neighbors and rural people across the country. A line from an essay he wrote for *Harper's* in 1985 is worth memorizing. The essay is "Holding to the Land: A Rancher's Sorrow," and the line goes: "In spite of a mushrooming rural population, our sense of isolation grows. We see ourselves as a few surrounded by many, with more on the way. We feel less secure, more vulnerable to violence from outside."

The fact is, the one strictly rural area surrounding Helena is growing like a weed and much of the valley development appears a bit reckless. From 1970 to 1980 Lewis and Clark County grew 29 percent, more than twice the rate of Montana as a whole. The Helena Valley accounted for more than 70 percent of that growth and charted a population explosion 20 times greater than the city of Helena. It is a problem all Helenans must face.

By the year 2000 the Helena Valley explosion is expected to mushroom and reach 21,000 people, a 62 percent increase over the current population. Some 3,000 more people are expected to establish 1,000 more households beyond the valley fringe while Helena is expected to grow by fewer than 5,000 residents.

Nearly all of the coming subdivisions will be built on Helena's dwindling agricultural land, the price of which no longer reflects its production value but rather its value as a ranchette dream factory. "In that sense we in agriculture are our own worst enemy," says rancher Scott Hibbard. The Hibbard family holds a prominent place in the history of Helena and of Montana, beginning in the 1860s. Scott Hibbard runs the portion of the family operation that is centered west of town. He is a member of the Montana Land Reliance and the Lewis and Clark County Planning Board. "From my perspective," Hibbard explains, "the real problem in the Helena Valley has been created by 'occasional sale'; people like me and other landowners who chop off a little tract here and another tract there, and pretty soon you've got sprawl and an unplanned mess in the valley."

There are several possible explanations for the disparity between growth rates in the city and the Helena Valley. Land in Helena has become increasingly more expensive to develop due to inflated land values and the escalating cost of city services, particularly water, and other sundry regulations that have made many city lots ineligible for federal housing programs. So, federal money has been much more plentiful in the Helena Valley. This, in addition to the desire to buy into the western myth by purchasing "rural" land— and the willingness of agriculture to sell off pieces of land, often to keep pace with the bills or to cash out and retire— has made the Helena Valley an increasingly more desirable place to live over the past 25 years.

Bill Diehl, a native Helenan and one of the city's major developers, worries that Helena's expensive development price has created a bargain

Rancher Scott Hibbard. JOHN REDDY

basement in the Helena Valley that could have an undesirable effect on the area's social character. "I think it is interesting that from 1970 to 1980 Helena grew by only 1,100 people, but the valley grew by 6,000. There was more than a 160 percent growth in the valley. There has got to be a reason for that. People don't want to choose [to live in a small house] out on the flats but they choose that over what's available in Helena. I think it's a serious problem for Helena— I think Helena has the danger of becoming very elite."

But elitism is a tag that has dogged Helena for more than a century. Helena banker William Whipps, who would become a mayor and banker in Kalispell, wrote in 1890 that he would "frankly say that I never liked Helena. Fishing was too far away to drive to by team for one thing, and I never saw so many brainless snobs converged on any one place before. Helena has always been noted for that. Not confined to men, but the women also."

And to some extent the tag has been justified, but possibly to a lesser degree than the sour Mr. Whipps would have us believe. Harriett Meloy, who has lived in Helena for more than 50 years and has been deeply involved in the town through various civic groups and as a staff member of the Montana Historical Society, agrees that there has always been a peculiar social structure evident in Helena.

"I've always thought there were two communities in Helena and that there always have been—westsiders and eastsiders," she says. "Believe me, that was the situation that contributed to the way you lived your life in Helena. But now there is the valley population, too. How do we mesh, or is it necessary to do that? I wonder if we shouldn't be more of a community than we are."

*   *   *

Perhaps too much can and has been made of schism between Helena and the Helena Valley. The populations do mesh, they are essentially one. Like the people who live in Helena, the city, those who choose to live in Helena, the valley, are comfortable in their choice and display the same ardent regional, state and city patriotism as their inner-city counterparts. They would live nowhere else. And in a pioneer zeal, they balk at rules and regulations that would crimp their country-living lifestyles.

"I don't know that the degree of difference in subdivision laws and land-use relations are that great between Washington, Idaho, Montana or South Dakota," says Bob Decker, who served as a Lewis and Clark County Commissioner for eight years before resigning in 1986. Decker, born in Havre, has lived in Helena since 1976. "There are different economic fuels burning in each area, but there are sprawl and occasional sales or the equivalent on mesas and in valleys across the northwest. I would say

Top: *Helena developer Bill Diehl.*
Left: *Harriett Meloy, former Montana Historical Society librarian.*
JOHN REDDY PHOTOS

there would have to strong legislative changes made to stop that; if indeed we want to stop it. We haven't yet."

Decker also has this to say: "I wouldn't affix that kind of theme, nor would I talk of Helena in those terms. If you talk about things like that, you're talking about a state of mind that's shared by a lot more people than the 30,000 who live in our area. It's shared by people across our state and the northwest and probably by most of our culture."

One thing is certain, Helenans do think about where and how they live and are at ease discussing among themselves their problems and expectations. Mary Wright, a native of the Midwest, Fulbright scholar, Montana Consumer Counsel attorney and co-owner of Big Sky Expeditions (a fly-fishing outfitter service), has noticed that sometimes Helenans are too hard on themselves, that their expectations may be too high.

"From the perspective of someone who has only been in Helena [since 1985], although I've been in Montana for five years, it seems to me [that people] are expecting a lot from Helena and expecting that Helena could somehow be different from almost every other town I've ever been in," she offers.

"There are not many towns that fulfill [those] kinds of expectations. It may be good to

Top: *The hearty Fighting Saints of Carroll College take to the football field at -20°.* RICK GRAETZ
Center: *Attorney Mary Wright.* JOHN REDDY
Left: *Former county commissioner Bob Decker.* JOHN REDDY

have those expectations, but it may not be good to think that this is a bad place because we can't fulfill them.

"From the point of view of a newcomer, Montana appealed to me greatly because it has a small population and I found it is simply not as materialistic a place as other places I have lived. And I like that. You can live here without having that materialism and those sorts of competitions complicating your life. You can focus on real things."

When life does get complicated, many Helenans turn to the mountains and clean rivers for recreation and for inspiration and they have fought hard to maintain that

resource. Helena is surrounded by the Helena National Forest and plans for how the forest will be used, according to Forest Supervisor Bob Gibson, are as closely monitored and examined by the public as any in the national forest system.

The Helena National Forest offers rich and varied opportunities for outdoor recreation, from extensive groomed snowmobile and cross-country ski trails to wilderness camping. In 1980, there were more than one quarter million visitor-days in the forest, a 35 percent increase in just five years. Helenans use the forest and it is no coincidence that the majority of the Helena for-

est's developed recreation sites are located on the Helena District, in close proximity to the state capital, the forest's largest urban area of influence.

Nearby, Helenans can hike two National Recreation Trails: Hanging Valley in the Big Belt Mountains in Trout Creek Canyon and the Mount Helena Trail No. 373, which connects Park City to Mount Helena. Portions of the Lewis and Clark National Historic Trail occur along the Missouri River near the Gates of the Mountains.

Some of the forest's most ardent visitors are hunters who live in and around Helena. About 48,000 elk-hunter recre-

Helena mayor Russ Ritter.
JOHN REDDY

ation days are charted in the Helena National Forest each season. Deer hunters account for approximately 37,000 visitor-days and bear hunters for 6,500 visitor-days.

In the Scapegoat Wilderness, north of Helena, some 239,000 acres lie within three national forests: the Lolo, the Lewis and Clark and the Helena. It is contiguous to the Bob Marshall Wilderness to the north. There are 82,958 acres of the Scapegoat on the Helena National Forest and recreational use in summer and fall is fairly heavy with the myriad of river- and lake-related activities associated with the Scapegoat and the adjoining Bob Marshall Wilderness.

These natural resources have made their way to the top of most value lists here, and that reliance is a Helena communal tie, but upon returning from hiking, skiing, fishing and hunting expeditions, many Helenans sorely want the style of social amenities—eclectic high-fashion shops, an array of restaurants, a spectrum of high-paying

jobs—that come only with a very wealthy, and trendy, local population.

That may be Helena's limiting factor, maybe to its benefit. If more forest and more agricultural land adjacent or integral to deer and elk populations is developed or consumed by subdivisions, what will we have lost? Where will the wildlife go? Where will Lake Helena's bald eagles go to winter? Will we still be able to focus on real things? Can Helena have both?

"I don't think so," Decker says. "The trend now is you're losing the attractiveness of Montana to the people with more money than time. Or is it more time than money? It looks to me as if they have both."

Decker pointed to the Smith River, a remote river that is becoming increasingly popular among recreationists in Helena, the rest of Montana,

and tourists from all points on the globe. It is also becoming increasingly popular among developers. Says Decker, "It's probably on the verge of being subdivided to the point where it won't be the Smith River you knew [five years ago]."

Helena Mayor Russell J. Ritter, a native of Helena, has heard the arguments before. "The future for us," he says, "despite what lifestyle we think we want, is dependent on an economy that has got to be pumped, got to be driven."

In Helena, and in Montana, the economy seems only to be "pumped" by industry that produces for sale out of state. Here that essentially means mining—gold mining. Currently two gold mines of note operate in the area. One substantial dig south of town—Montana Tunnels, near Wicks—and the St. Joe's placer mine, located off North Montana, on the northern city limits. At St. Joe's, miners pan essentially the same gravels the Four Georgians did. There are prospects for another large gold mining operation being developed near Winston.

Looking east from the top of the Civic Center. From this vantage point, it is easy to see how the design of the Steamboat Block (left center, facing intersection) matches the name. RICK GRAETZ

Left: Mining speculator B.H. Tatem's home dates from about 1890. RICK GRAETZ

But, like it or not, with regard to the mining industry, local history is prologue. "Since we've got a couple of mines started," Ritter surmised, "you can find as many people who disagree with that industry as those who invite it."

That debate, too, is an essential Helena motif. "When you get to Helena," Decker says, "the provincialism acquires a political aspect. It's the state capital. In Helena we talk about the policies of the state, the legislature and we're bombarded by it all the time. Its regulations and government and our natural connections to the national capital.

"In that way, our provincialism seems to be unique. It's not easily attached to other areas. For instance, in eastern Montana, when I leave Sidney and reach Miles City, the people are pretty much the same; I can almost start up a conversation wherever I left off and feel at home. In Helena, we're more theoretical about things."

In Jim Harrison's poem, "The Theory & Practice of Rivers," there is this observation:

"In New York and L.A.
 you don't want to see, hear, smell,
  and you only open your mouth in restaurants.
 At night you touch people with rock-hard skins.

I'm trying to become alert enough to live."

In contrast, Helena is a place where all of one's senses can be put to good use. It is a place that makes you want to be alert enough to live. Bill Skidmore, the city editor of the Helena *Independent Record,* has been a newsman in Helena for nearly two decades. He has chronicled Helena's Urban Renewal era, the environmental and development flaps, and has kept pace with the town's changing character as only a newspaper reporter can.

Reporters are known for their cynicism, yet when Skidmore was asked for thoughts on his life here, he spoke with a sense of melancholy that comes with deep affection.

"Although I'm certainly not alone in coming from Wisconsin, I headed west as a very young man just out of college and came to gain experience in the newspaper business with the idea that I'd move on to a metro paper. Having children and having lived here for several years I made a choice that I was going to stay. You continue to rationalize—you

Bill Skidmore of the Independent Record. JOHN REDDY

want to raise your kids in a small town and when I go back to Wisconsin there is something missing on the horizon.

"Anyway, this is where I am and this is where I enjoy living, even if there is a lack of economic opportunity. One person recently suggested to me that we live in the American equivalent of a Third World nation and if you want to live here you pay a premium. If you want to live near the mountains and the forests, you have to pay a price. I think a lot of people have done that—not only the ones who grew up here, but the ones who have moved here. I grew up in a town not much bigger than Helena, a place where people didn't say 'Hi!' on the street like they do in Helena, Montana. It's a pretty friendly place, and I think there is something special about that."

One suspects there are at least 30,000 other people, from politicos rubbing elbows in the Windbag on Last Chance Gulch, to ranchers branding calves in the far reaches of the valley, who feel the same way.

Top: The Last Chance Stampede at the end of July combines rodeo and the Lewis and Clark County fair. GARRY WUNDERWALD
Right: Great Divide Ski Area (formerly Belmont) near Marysville. RICK GRAETZ

9 MOUNT HELENA

I can't count the times I've seen deer while hiking Mount Helena. I usually see them browsing on bitter brush in a slalom-timbered drainage on the south-facing slope. But I have a friend, a native of Malibu, who in winter has taken to surfing down the mountain on a boogie board, and he swears to have once swooped down on a massive mule deer that was resting in a small quarry just 100 yards from the mountain park's residential boundary. When I worked downtown, through the office window, I'd often spot great mule deer silhouetted against the autumn sky feeding on the long pleat of the southeast slope.

Lately, and only in winter, I've taken to following the snow-packed game trails that crisscross the hill through the timber and out again and I'm always impressed at the richness of the tracks. In the back of the mountain there are elk, and deeper, heading west toward Colorado Gulch and Black Mountain, there are moose and mountain lions and black bears. And no roads. There is, however, a dandy trail.

On June 8, 1979, 2^1/$_2$ miles of Mount Helena city park trail were joined to 4^1/$_2$ miles of Helena National Forest trail. The marriage created the Mt. Helena Trail, the 250th addition to the U.S. Department of the Interior's National Recreation Trail System.

The Mt. Helena Trail, No. 373, winds its way down from the mountain's 5,468' summit, leaves the city park and enters the Helena National Forest leading you west toward the Continental Divide. There it traverses an open grassy ridge and continues along a geologic fold affording the hiker wide

Kara Graetz hiking on Mt. Helena, the massive city park. RICK GRAETZ

Facing page: Colorado Gulch west of Helena.
Below: *The view across Spring Meadow Lake State Park on Helena's west side includes the limestone cliffs atop Mt. Helena.*
RICK GRAETZ PHOTOS

views of the Prickly Pear Valley and Helena's back country,
some of which still bears the
pocked scars of the mining
heydays.

The trail ends at Nelson
Gulch, but the stout-hearted
equipped with a simple Forest
Service map can continue
through the roadless Black
Mountain country. While
walking along the narrow trail
through old-growth timber,
watch for large stones that
have been overturned by black
bears searching for grubs.
Look up at the clawed bark of
aspen and limber pine for sure
signs of black-bear activity.
The elk are secure here and
have made it a breeding
ground vital to elk populations
in the Ten Mile drainage. And
unlike places like Wolf Creek,
where there are now no
wolves, and Grizzly Gulch,
where there are now no grizzly
bears,

you still can find moose near
Moose Creek.

You can end the hike on the
other side of Moose Creek
Pass, just 20 miles west of Helena, but through back country
hundreds of years removed
from civilization. Some have
come to call it "Helena's Wilderness," but the "wilderness"
presently is threatened by a
scheduled Forest Service
timber sale.

From the fringe of Helena's
neighborhoods to a tiny camp-
ground near Rimini, sits a
wildlife and scenic paradise
that ought not be destroyed for
a couple of thousand board feet
of wood to be sold as if at a fire
sale. Here is a tiny wilderness:
a microcosm of
Helena's

rich historic ecosystem. If you
road it, you blow it for good.
It's that simple. The security
for moose, elk and black bears
will disappear. It is such a
special place, here in the midst
of the Capital City, and it is as
environmentally secure for its
small herds of wildlife as is the
gold that is surely still in the
hills. Somehow, it should be
secured forever.

Funny, but it was gold, big
game and security that had
prompted a few prospectors to
venture onto Mount Helena itself in 1863, 10 months before
the historic discovery of gold in
Last Chance
Gulch. But
even

those visitors were apparently
on the mountain *after* Henry
"Gold Tom" Thomas, the
solitary miner who sank the
first shaft of record in Montana.

Gold Tom was different. His
one partner, while prospecting
down Montana City way, put a
Colt .45 to his own head. The
gruesome suicide compelled
Gold Tom to take the rugged
individualist ethos to heart. At
a time when most prospectors
were joining together like
musketeers to expedite the
gut-busting digging, Gold Tom
worked alone. After his
partner's suicide, late in the
summer of 1862, Gold Tom
was sluicing east of Helena
and finding little gold. But the
exquisite big game in Prickly
Pear Valley agreed with his
state of mind. It seemed a good
place, with few distractions
and plenty of game. He eventually wandered north and
often made camp at the hot
springs where Col. Charles A.
Broadwater later built his
Moorish hotel and natatorium.
Gold Tom sank shafts in many
of Helena's gold-bearing
gulches—including Last

Chance—but for him the valley's big game was far more
accessible than the gulches'
gold.

A year after the suicide of
Gold Tom's partner, and 10
months before the Four Geor-

gians found gold in Last
Chance Gulch, James Oldham
and his partner camped near
the base of Mount Helena and
watched the elk grazing on the
bunchgrass and rough fescue.
They kept watching the elk

and finally decided that a couple of good steaks would taste far better than the sourdough biscuits and lard that was on tap for supper.

But elk are elk. The two chased the herd over Mount Helena's summit, and the mountain and the elk eventually beat the breath out of the would-be hunters. On the descent through the old-growth timber, stout pine and fir, Oldham and his partner took what has become the most popular Mount Helena foot trail. It's now known as the 1906 trail, in honor of a reforestation project initiated by a group of 75 or so civic minded folks who, at $25 a throw, became life members in a "Helena Improvement Society."

Yet, even in 1863 the trail skirted the mountain's distinguished limestone cliffs, bypassing a wonderful soot-blackened cave the locals call "Devil's Kitchen."

It's not as foreboding as the cave through which old Indian Joe chased Tom Sawyer and Becky Thatcher, but for generations it was the destination of every pre-teen secret society that Helena's kids could conjure. Oddly, though, there are few kids on the hill these days. Mostly it's hikers, athletes and naturalists using the mountain for spiritual and physical renewal. Anyhow, on his descent Oldham explored the cavern and found a package wrapped in brown paper. On the package, the note read:

"Dear tom: me and the boys have gone to bannack. we have left some flour and coffy and bacon. the sugar got wet and is split. the indians stole the two pack horses."

There was also a cooking outfit in the package. Chances are good that the package was left for Gold Tom by some miners who, at Tom's direction, headed up the mountain to prospect and were told to use the cavern as a safe camp. Chances are also good that Gold Tom had no intention of joining "me and the boys," but that's something neither they nor Oldham could have known. Oldham and his partner left the provisions in Devil's Kitchen and returned to their own camp—above today's intersection of Broadway and Park—a literal stone's throw from the spot where the Georgians would later strike gold.

These boys were not blessed with luck. They found no gold in Last Chance Gulch. Failed to bag an elk. Then, the next day, while unpacking the horses after a half-day trek to what would later become Confederate Gulch—where in 1865 the largest placer fortune in Montana was discovered—"a shower of bullets fell in our midst," Oldham wrote, "accompanied by a series of the most demonic yells...ever heard. We were attacked by Indians."

The pack horses were shot and Oldham and his partner high-tailed it on their hastily rigged saddle horses across the Prickly Pear Valley keeping the Indians at bay, cleverly they thought, with their breech-loaded Sharp .50-caliber rifles. The Indians, however, probably didn't care

about the reach of Oldham's rifles. With the pack animals left for dead, the Indians would certainly have been satisfied with chasing off the intruders and packing away the goods left behind. And the Indians probably packed the stuff away on the horses stolen from "me and the boys."

But poor Oldham hid in the valley's thickets for a full day—without food. The fol-

lowing midnight he and his partner crept back to Mount Helena, killed an antelope for supper and went up for the cache of flour, bacon and coffee left for Gold Tom in Devil's Kitchen. And it was, of course, still there.

Mount Helena today probably looks about as it did when Oldham was gobbling Gold Tom's grub 125 years ago, but

its short history, like Montana's own, is rife with exploitation and ecological neglect.

It has survived fire, overgrazing and deforestation as well as years of off-road vehicle abuse that still, unfortunately and unlawfully, sometimes poses a problem.

In the 1860s, as soon as gold was discovered in the gulch, Mount Helena became Hele-

Autumn color, autumn snow on the road from Unionville toward Colorado Mountain. RICK GRAETZ

na's timber bank. The miners and merchants denuded the hill for cabin logs and mine timbers, sluice boxes, flumes, fuel and bridges. Then horses, cattle and sheep were put to pasture on the hill. When the hill was gnawed raw, a few thousand goats were turned loose on it. It was a modern range conservationist's worst nightmare.

In 1898, a group of Helena citizens formed the first "Helena Improvement Society," just one of the long line of Helena "boom your town" campaigns prompted by the publisher of the local newspaper. Their overall objective was to put some spit and polish on the town and acquire the mountain as a city park. U.S. government land as well as private mining parcels were donated, deeded and purchased for the city with funds raised by the society.

By 1903, two years after a week-long July fire ravaged the mountain, the determined society built the first "official" foot trail to the summit with funds raised during the winter. The folks even built

The annual Montana Traditional Jazz Festival, inaugurated in 1983, brings Dixieland bands— and fans—from throughout the West to Helena on the weekend preceding the Fourth of July. DARLENE DURGAN

A Prickly Pear Valley wheatfield with the Belt Mountains on the horizon. RICK GRAETZ

wooden rest benches every 1,000 feet. For the first time ever, there was a movement afoot for people to use the hill for recreation, a progressive reform movement that was symbolized across the nation in the persona of Teddy Roosevelt, who himself paid Helena a visit in 1903.

The following year a shelter house was built on the summit and torchlight processions became a common mountain ritual.

In 1905, *Technical World Magazine* called the Mount Helena park endeavor "the strangest and most interesting park project undertaken in this country," primarily because the U.S. Forest Service agreed to help reforest the barren hill with 10,000 ponderosa pines and 20,000 Douglas firs. The two-year-old trees were planted in the spring of 1906 and by August none of the young trees had survived the dry, hot summer. Trees were replanted in October and most survived the winter.

For the next 60 years not much attention was paid to the great mountain park. In the 1940s, the world's first Special Services Force, the precursor of the Green Berets, trained in Helena and used the mountain for drills, but over the years the mountain was generally abused. Motorcycle trails scarred its face and really accounted for its major use, or abuse. Horse owners, too, leased the park from the city for pasture land. It was pretty much a mess until 1972 when the Save Mount Helena Committee rallied to once again restore the hill.

The grassroots committee succeeded in getting the city to cancel the horse-grazing leases, stopped off-road vehicle use and generally got the city interested in its mountain. That committee's accomplishments are no less important than the work of the original Helena Improvement Society.

In 1984 yet another grassroots group, "The Friends of Mount Helena," emerged to stop the city and Lewis and Clark County from erecting a shared communications tower near the top of Mount Helena. It was a bitter and often ugly battle, but in the end an aesthetic compromise was reached that did not limit emergency communication. The tower was erected, but it is far shorter than original plans called for and thus needs no flashing red light, which would mar the handsome hill.

The Friends of Mount Helena are still loosely organized and have, with the help of the City of Helena Parks Department, posted directional signs on the park's trailheads.

But now is the time to look beyond the peak of Mount Helena and to the green timbered hills to the west. By 1990 those rolling green hills could be badly scarred with logging roads and clearcuts. Mount Helena's sister, Black Mountain, also needs a friend.

10 CANYON FERRY, MISSOURI RIVER

It was originally a spot on the Missouri River where John Oakes ferried across prospectors who were seeking easy access to their claims in the Big Belt Mountains. In 1865, the miners called it the canyon ferry.

It has become the most-used state-run recreation site in Montana and, next to the mountains, the most dominant geographic feature in the valley. It's still called Canyon Ferry.

In 1889, the Missouri River Power Company built a 30'-high dam across the river, about one mile upstream from the one that would be completed in 1954 by the Bureau of Reclamation. In 1957, the Bureau of Land Management agreed to allow the state parks division to manage the site and today the Montana Department of Fish, Wildlife and Parks administers the 8,000 acres that surround the impoundment. In all, at Canyon Ferry there are 25 recreational areas, eight boat ramps, 14 camping areas, five day-use areas and one group reservation site, a tent-only area and four areas accessible only by boat.

Residents of cities within a 150-mile radius regularly visit the area for camping and lake fishing. Trolling is the method of choice on the lake for anglers after large brown and rainbow trout. In fall, waterfowl hunters build their blinds on the south end of the lake and in the surrounding grain fields for consistently good gunning for ducks and geese.

The waterfowl are thriving on the south end of the lake. A series of dikes has created 1,900 acres of marshland that have aided nesting and breeding waterfowl and provide

Above: *Canyon Ferry Lake, the reservoir created by Canyon Ferry Dam on the Missouri River.*
Below: *The Spokane Hills at the eastern side of the Prickly Pear Valley.* RICK GRAETZ PHOTOS

resting and feeding sites for migrant birds in the spring and fall. Small islands were constructed and vegetative cover was planted to improve the habitat. Even the reluctant wood duck is making a seasonal home at Canyon Ferry.

With a shoreline of 76 miles, outlined with osprey and eagle nests, Canyon Ferry Lake

extends from Townsend to the dam, a distance of about 25 miles. At its widest spot, the lake stretches across the valley for eight miles and comes to a 1,000'-wide bottleneck at the dam. The lake, located between portions of the Helena National Forest, is bounded on both sides by rolling, pine-covered hills. There are willows and cottonwoods on the bottoms. Bunchgrass, juniper and sage—favored by the roving herds of antelope—cover the rolling plains land. Evergreens and mountain shrubs grow on the steep lands at the north end of the lake.

The area is rife with mining lore and prehistoric sites. Pictographs have been found on the cliffs of Hellgate Canyon on the east shore, and tipi rings have been discovered throughout the area.

Farther downstream is Hauser Lake. Its dam originally was constructed by Samuel T. Hauser in 1908 to supply the Butte and Anaconda mines with hydroelectric power. Now owned by the Montana Power Company, it is

a popular recreation site for boaters and anglers.

River anglers fish below the dam for good-sized trout while lake anglers troll the waters for heavy kokanee salmon. Black Sandy Beach Recreation Area, a mere 20 miles from Helena, is a popular destination for campers.

The last in the string of Missouri River dams near Helena also is named for an early-day Helena capitalist: Anton M. Holter. Holter Lake is less known for its fishing than for where the Missouri River's "blue ribbon" trout fishing begins. From Wolf Creek to the Dearborn River, the Missouri River is one of the best trout fisheries in Montana. Access is a cinch and it is well used by local fly fishermen who have learned to keep mum about the glory holes on the big river.

The Holter Lake area also is home to the Beartooth Wildlife Management Area, a sprawling game range set aside for deer, elk, big horn sheep and mountain goats.

Top: *The town of Canyon Ferry on the Missouri River was covered by Canyon Ferry Lake in the 1950s. Today only the town's hilltop cemetery is visible above water.* COURTESY JEAN BAUCUS

Right: *The Big Belt Mountains edging the Prickly Pear Valley.* RICK GRAETZ

11 THE ELKHORNS

oday the volcanic Elkhorns, drained from the high, trout-rich Tizer Basin by Crow Creek, form the lushest, wettest basin-and-range island in this arid region. Helena is surrounded by wonderful wildlife, but the Elkhorns are Helena's wildlife wonderland. Best known for its uniquely managed elk herd, the area also is home to black bears, fat moose in the low bogs and mountain goats that can be found near the high peaks.

The Elkhorns and their Prickly Pear Valley environs are believed to be a Great North Trail killing ground of animals as big as the prehistoric mammoth and the half-ton horned bison. The hunters are identified by finely crafted projectile points and are known as Folsom and Clovis peoples, both named for paleontological sites located in New Mexico.

The Clovis peoples typically killed the huge animals with spears thrown with a sling. Their projectile points were large and had a characteristic flute or groove cut up from the base for easy attachment to a spear. Clovis peoples followed the mammoth migrations as the American Indian followed the bison.

Folsom peoples are believed to be descended from the Clovis peoples. They followed the horned bison and typically used smaller, fully fluted projectiles, painstakingly chipped to razor edges.

In the Elkhorns, at Indian Creek near Townsend, undisturbed Clovis and Folsom sites have been discovered. The sites were probably camps and butchering spots along the Great North Trail, for the fluted projectiles of both Clovis and Folsom peoples have been unearthed. The Clovis pro-

Top: *Beaver Pond on Hope Creek, Helena National Forest.* JOHN REDDY
Left: *The Elkhorn foothills from near Winston.* RICK GRAETZ

Right: *Elkhorn Peak.*
Below: *The Elkhorns as seen from the South Hills above Helena.*
RICK GRAETZ PHOTOS

jectiles were fashioned of quartzite mined from the Limestone Hills. Ironically, the sites were found because 100 years of mining invited a more cerebral breed of "miners" to comb and dust the placer channels in search of ancient man.

Folsom Complex projectile points have been excavated in original, or undisturbed, context at only two Montana sites. Indian Creek is one and the MacHaffie Site, sitting under a housing development at Montana City, is the other. The MacHaffie site, named for a

local amateur archaeologist, is presently being studied by professional archaeologists trying to gather ancient data before it is further disturbed by water wells, septic systems, powerlines and other accoutrements of modern camps.

The Elkhorns also have a modern history. Silver mining predominated. On the Cretaceous/Tertiary fence, when the hot springs and magma and volcanoes heaved and belched, silver sulfides were deposited. Over the eternities, erosion concentrated the deposits and through the cool alchemy of rainwater the sulfides were transformed to heavier silver chloride. With every rain, more silver sulfide would be transformed and the true silver deposit would grow like an interest-bearing mutual fund.

Geologists call the lodes "supergene enrichments." Parts of the Elkhorns were stocked with a few supergene enrichments and the scars of mining camps appear near old claims.

Elkhorn, with its school, church, hotel, stores, saloons and brothels, was the most successful and sophisticated mining town that emerged. A thick ore vein, not a simple supergene enrichment that was less mined than plucked from the earth, kept Elkhorn in high-society delicacies and imported cigars for a short but harried time that seemed to end too soon.

The Elkhorn Lode was discovered in 1869 by Peter Wys, a Swiss immigrant. Six years later one of Helena's best known capitalists, Anton Holter, developed the mine in a

big way. More than $14 million in silver was carried out of the mine, and Elkhorn, with its 2,500 inhabitants in 1889, boasted a railroad spur to Boulder. In 1890, the Sherman Silver Purchase Act passed and the federal treasury was bound by law to purchase 4.5 million ounces of silver for monthly coinage. The Elkhorns rioted with crazy wealth. Yet in three years, the silver boom and Elkhorn began to die. Compared to gold, silver proved to be an artificial, untrustworthy standard and the dollar plummeted on the international exchange.

Elkhorn is now a ghost town and the area—known as the Elkhorn Wildlife Management Unit—has been returned to wildlife.

Environmentalists, however, have continued to keep a close watch on the Elkhorns because mining and timber interests still may be permitted limited development opportunities in the lush mountains.

Top: *Main Street in Elkhorn, a boomtown when silver prices were high in the 1870s and '80s.* EDWARD M. REINIG PHOTO, MONTANA HISTORICAL SOCIETY
Left: *Unionville, surrounded by Helena National Forest.* RICK GRAETZ
Facing page: *Park Lake in the Helena National Forest.* JOHN REDDY

72

12 GATES OF THE MOUNTAINS WILDERNESS

by Rick Graetz

When you look out toward the northern horizon from Helena, the foothills and lower peaks of the Rocky Mountain front range seem to blend together in a continuously forested belt, separating the Helena Valley from the prairie farther north. The distant view is deceiving. Out there in those hills, the big Missouri has cut its path through the limestone, leaving towering walls that Lewis and Clark called The Gates of the Mountains. About 10 miles to the east of this formation, man has carved a scenic road along Beaver Creek. It too is bordered by spectacular cliffs. In between lies Helena's backyard wilderness, The Gates of the Mountains.

The high peaks that characterize Glacier National Park, the Madison Range, the Beartooth and other Montana wilderness areas are missing. In their place, The Gates of the Mountains offers picturesque limestone escarpments and gentle forested mountains.

At 28,562 acres, The Gates of the Mountains is Montana's smallest wilderness area (the largest is the Selway-Bitterroot at 1,238,355 acres). At this writing, a bill is being proposed in Congress by members of our delegation that would add 10,000 acres on the western and southern borders of the wilderness to be known as the Big Log Addition. The western segment would include the cliffs along the Missouri River. Its size, accessibility and easy walking make it an ideal place for family trips and for those new to backpacking.

Top: Figure 8 road—seen here near York—is named for the shape of its loop through Gates of the Mountains area.
Left: Susan Hanson hiking in the Belt Mountains, Gates of the Mountains Wilderness.
RICK GRAETZ PHOTOS

Below: *Just right of center are the "Gates," where the Missouri River seems, as one approaches by water, to dead-end against solid rock walls.* RICK GRAETZ

A wilderness experience in every way, The Gates of the Mountains offers an excellent trail system leading through high open meadows, beautiful forest land and narrow gorges cut by streams. Several of the higher mountains are easily climbed from points along the various trails. Elk, deer, bears, mountain lions, mountain goats, coyotes and golden eagles frequent the area. In the spring the meadows, open slopes and forest floor display an array of wildflowers. Summer brings a bright green moss-like phlox covering to much of the limestone outcroppings as well as to the lower parts of the cliffs.

The trails are simple to negotiate and no one trip through the country requires more than two days. For the strong hiker, a one-day 16-mile walk crosses the area.

Human use in the Gates of the Mountains Wilderness is low, and the opportunity for solitude, high. The Forest Service estimates that no more than 800 people visit the Gates in any one year, and most of that use is for hiking and hunting. There are 42 miles of

trails and about 36 miles of them are maintained. Water and horse feed are scarce. The Hunter's Gulch and Refrigerator Canyon trails have stock unloading ramps and hitching rails.

The most popular trip commences at Refrigerator Canyon, about 13 miles north of York, and comes out at Meriwether landing, on the Missouri River, some 16 miles away. Refrigerator Canyon is a dramatic sight. A deep narrow gorge just a little wider than a horse escapes the sunlight and funnels winds, resulting in a temperature many degrees colder than outside the canyon. Moors Creek flows through Refrigerator Canyon. The trail passes through the forest winding its way up the mountainside, gaining elevation slowly. The midway point—about eight miles in and usually the overnight camp—is Bear Prairie. A high meadow that slopes southward, Bear Prairie offers water, good views and a chance to climb 7,443' Candle Mountain by way of a game trail. Candle Mountain is the

high point northeast of the meadow. From its summit, the Helena Valley, Rocky Mountain Front, Bob Marshall Wilderness and Tobacco Root Mountains are visible. Those who know their mountains will also be able to identify the Flint Creek and Mission ranges. From Bear Prairie the trail eventually drops sharply down through Meriwether Canyon to the Missouri. "Gates" tour boats stop several times a day at Meriwether so hikers can finish with a pleasant boat ride. This trip, of course, requires a car at each end and knowledge of the boat schedule.

For those not wishing to take the boat, another trail from Bear Prairie goes down Big Log Gulch to Hunters Gulch and out to Nelson, about five miles from Refrigerator Canyon. Two cars would be helpful here as well. The Big Log Gulch trail takes off downhill at Kennedy Springs and is well marked, as are all Gates of the Mountains routes.

The northern portions of the wilderness are reached from Wolf Creek via a road that runs along Holter Lake to the Beartooth Game Ranch. Two roads, one up Willow Creek and the other along Elkhorn Creek, lead to trails heading

Bear Prairie in Gates of the Mountains Wilderness. RICK GRAETZ

into the wilderness. The Willow Creek trail allows access to Mann Gulch and an overlook of the Missouri River and Gates of the Mountains. Mann Gulch is the sight of the disastrous 1948 forest fire that took the lives of 13 smokejumpers. This area is a good place to sight deer and eagles. The trail is pleasan; the area's openness allows good vistas.

The same road goes to trail 260, a route that runs along the northern perimeter, with a steep trail going south to Bear Prairie and a trail that winds up in the vicinity of 7,980' Moors Mountain—the highest peak in the Gates of theMountain Wilderness, in its northeastern corner. Trails up Porcupine and Dry Gulch and creeks, reached from the Beaver Creek Road, lead to Moors Mountain as well.

A full-day trip is the loop trail that goes up Spring Gulch and reaches the Missouri River via Fields Gulch. Another trail from the river goes back to the starting point. This area is found in the southwestern part of the wilderness. It is best reached from Nelson on the Beaver Creek road out of York.

The Gates of the Mountains is void of lakes; however, streams and springs throughout the area provide water. Willow, Moors, Porcupine and

Above: In Gates of the Mountains Wilderness. RICK GRAETZ

Viewed from above, the Gates of the Mountains reveal the illusion they work on Missouri River travelers. RICK GRAETZ

Hunters creeks are reliable for water. Small springs such as Kennedy, Bear Prairie and Turnout also are dependable.

Although the peaks in this wilderness aren't very high, they provide the opportunity— if not on the same scale as elsewhere in Montana—for the hiker to experience the thrill of climbing a mountain. All the peaks are easily climbed and provide excellent views. The highest mountains in the wilderness are: Moors Mountain 7,980', Candle Mountain 7,443', Willow Mountain 7,190', Cap Mountain 6,760' and Sacajawea Mountain 6,439'.

The Forest Service map of The Gates of the Mountains Wilderness shows all the above-mentioned trails and roads and points out places to get water. The Helena National Forest Supervisor's office and the Helena Ranger District office, both located in Helena, have this map.

The Gates of the Mountains offers perhaps the longest visiting season of any of Montana's wilderness areas. Owing to its lower elevation and the semi-arid climate of the surrounding area, the snow is often gone by mid-May and trail-blocking snows usually hold off until October. The flowers are at their best in June and early July. Early autumn displays beautiful color in the lower elevations and up in the meadows.

Most of the access roads are closed by snow in winter; however, for those willing to ski the extra miles, the Gates offers excellent ski touring.

Call it Helena's backyard wilderness, Helena's family wilderness or the Gates of the Mountains—whatever name you prefer, the main concern is to experience it. It can best be described as a very nice encounter; not something that will overwhelm you like the high alpine country, but rather a place that will prove well worth the effort of exploring it.

The Holter Lumber Company operation on Wegner Creek, 1885, near the present site of Holter Dam. COURTESY JEAN BAUCUS

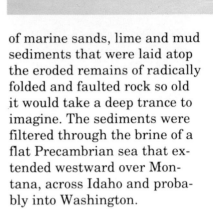

13 GEOLOGY

A lot of things are matters of timing. Timing and inevitability.

—*Hal Borland*

The Big Belt Mountains, Helena's horizon, are a morning range. The sun struggles to lift itself over the Big Belt hills morning after morning, blasting day into the valley long before its first glint burns from the dark summits.

Above: *The Great Divide Ski Area rises above Marysville.*
Top: *Looking to the west and south of Helena from Granite Butte.* RICK GRAETZ PHOTOS

As the day progresses the Big Belts turn as solemn and patriarchal as a grandfather. Look out to the Big Belt Mountains. Squat and muscled, with few peaks above timberline, the Big Belts harbor the region's senior rocks and sit atop the remnants of annihilated mountain ranges eroded flat, over and over again, in deep, deep time.

Portions of the hills represent unfathomably old sheets of marine sands, lime and mud sediments that were laid atop the eroded remains of radically folded and faulted rock so old it would take a deep trance to imagine. The sediments were filtered through the brine of a flat Precambrian sea that extended westward over Montana, across Idaho and probably into Washington.

The Belt Formation marks time's beginning in Helena, but like the morning light that floods the valley before sunrise, time was way before the Belt Formation. Way before.

Helena, just over a billion years ago, was the flat floor of a shallow sea that would deliver few plant fossils and no animal fossils. Not a whole lot of living going on back then. It was oppressively hot, with near-boiling seas and never-ending hot rains. The evidence of shallow mudflats—primitive algae fossils, ripples trapped for eternity on the dark rock, mud cracks and casts of salt crystals—can be found throughout the strata.

Geologists also suspect that Helena's Precambrian seafloor kept dropping as the sea

tion rock. There are islands of Belt rock immediately west and east of the city. And the formation is Helena's bedrock.

Five uneven layers distinguish the Belt Series in the Prickly Pear Valley environs. The five layers comprise about 12,000 feet in thickness in some places. Four of the five formations are shale, the exception is a blue-gray limestone named for Helena that is nearly a mile thick in spots.

The quarrymen of the 1880s called the Helena-formation rock "bastard limestone" because its soft, crystalline composition rendered it incapable of being converted into quicklime when burnt in their kilns.

The Belt Series rock forms the first rung in the fairly simple geologic ladder Helena has ascended. The valley geology is neat and orderly.

depths remained quite stable, an irony explained by plate tectonics, the theory of continental drift that maintains that the earth's crust is laid on plates wandering about the globe not unlike amusement park crash cars. As the plates move in opposing directions, great ocean basins are left in the gaps. That might account for the Helena-area seafloor falling into the abyss but because the Precambrian sea was weighted with so much muck, the sediments were laid nearly as fast as the floor sank.

Much of the northwest-to-southeast rim of the valley—from the Big Belts to the Spokane Hills—is composed of that muck now turned to the characteristically soft shales of the Precambrian Era's somewhat mysterious Belt Forma-

Oxbow Bend on the Missouri River. TOM CORDINGLEY

The Sleeping Giant, landmark of the Prickly Pear Valley's northern horizon. MARK THOMPSON

But the area has been poked and jabbed and tortured by a variety of hard rock acts and not a little geologic sleight of hand. And that has been Helena's fortune and misfortune. A person more attuned to mythology than science could see the cupped hands of Pluto offering Helena the mineral riches of the underworld, an invitation later violently revoked by quaking hills that leveled the elaborate shrines built to honor his gifts of silver and gold. I often imagine the Sleeping Giant could be Pluto, the terrible but just Greek god. When the North Hill burned so fiercely in the dry summer of 1984, the giant appeared to sleep so soundly. But he may have a right not to pay much mind to the destruction. He will be here when we are gone. And eventually he too will be eroded away. The Giant's stillness is a reminder that it has taken eons for the earth to manufacture the riches extracted here and eons more to squeeze them into the rock.

Helena was an awfully rich town once. Millions in real money, millions more in promises, and still more millions in schemes. By 1890 boosters called Helena "The Queen City of the Rockies." The town was as opulent as the valley was desolate. Capitalism had run amok.

Consider that Thomas Edison did not flip the switch to inaugurate the commercial transmission of electric power in New York City until September 4, 1882. The young daughter of a Helena capitalist had switched on the dynamo here a week earlier. In 1890 boosters boasted that more millionaires per capita lived in Helena than in any other city in the world.

The eons, too, have been quite generous to Helena. About 530 million years ago, following the hot and muddy Precambrian Era, the sea retreated, leaving the land low and dry. Helena was on the beach. The land would sometimes heave and rise farther above sea level but in time the force of erosion flattened it down to a lower relief.

When the sea again invaded the region, it left 300 feet of sand sediments. The first waves' cargo of sand pebbles was laid atop the gently tilted Precambrian shale and for millions of years fine sand was deposited on the pebbles. The rock is distinguished by its hard, fine-grained quartzite, the metamorphosed product of sandstone.

The sea that brought the Flathead sands to Helena also carried the planet's first significant signs of animal life. Other portions of the continent had been teeming with marine brachiopods and trilobites for 30 million years before Helena acquired its first sea shell. There is a moral there for Helena teenagers who are convinced that hip fashions hit Capitol Hill Mall a light year after flashing on both coasts.

Helena wears the 540-million-year-old Flathead quartzite like a powerlifter's belt. The comparatively thin but rugged formation appears to hold a conglomeration of younger shales and limestones from spilling off the slopes of Mt. Helena and Mt. Ascension and onto the Precambrian shale of the Belt Series.

Thanks to the mountain building that occurred about 500 million years after the Flathead sands were deposited, Montana's first Paleozoic Era formation is easy to follow.

Look toward Mt. Helena's far west side. About a third of the way up the hill, there is an abrupt change in the landscape. The gently rising hill is met by a low ridge that often becomes a steeper and rougher segment of the mountain. The ridge is the remnant of com-

pressed marine sandstone that would bend but would not easily break, arching from below where the earth's crust began to fold when the North American plate, floating leisurely westward, hit the

great Pacific Ocean crustal plate. The effects were felt locally about 78 million years ago. Upon the late-Cretaceous collision, the North American plate began to crumple. It marked the first phase in a

In the Big Belt Mountains, looking toward the Prickly Pear Valley.
RICK GRAETZ

long series of events that twice built the Rocky Mountains and eventually helped to push and fold that resisting Flathead formation around the girth of Mt. Helena.

Following the formation east, the ridge breaks radically and falls back to the south where it intersects Last Chance Gulch. The ridge continues its southeast course across Davis Street where it is intruded upon and reduced by a mass of granite. Undaunted, the defiant ridge stands up again and virtually runs parallel to Interstate 15 nearly to Montana City.

Mt. Helena, from the low ridge to its Hasmark Dolomite summit, is a stack of fine Cambrian-time rocks. Most prominently, the great white bluffs of the mountain are a Meagher limestone.

The entire mountain sags down toward the south. Some geologists think the southward dip of Helena's sedimentary formations is a result of the magmatic activity of the Boulder Batholith. They theorize that as the batholith cooked and softened nearby sedimentary rock, Helena and its

mountains actually began to sink into it.

The Paleozoic, the age of life, was a good, lasting age. It is all around us. The sea regularly moved in and out, irregularly across Montana, sometimes reaching Helena

and sometimes not. But after Cambrian time 105 million years went by without a trace.

Time begins to be charted again in Helena with the disposition of the sands that formed the pervasive Madison formation. The rock harbors

84

Red Mountain towers over the Ten Mile Creek drainage and the town of Rimini. RICK GRAETZ

the sea lily and feather star fossils that are in limestone of similar age all around the world.

A portion of the formation, the gray to black limestone beds separated by sheaths of shale, is the cherty rock, the flint prehistoric visitors used to fashion weapons. The top of the formation is a very massive limestone that has become a white marble in places.

The Madison limestone was laid in Mississippian time, about 350 million years ago. When it began, all of Montana was under the sea and the first 790 feet of the Madison formation was deposited. The period ended with Montana primarily emerged.

About the time the upper Madison rock was being deposited, Helena was tropical, possibly as close to the equator then as San Jose, Costa Rica is today. The lowest portion of the rock is that "bastard limestone" of no use to Helena's early quarrymen. But the tropics left behind a museum of primitive fossils and a significant fossil-fuel storage capacity that has been tapped

with considerable success on the eastern plains.

And get this, tropical sea is in our sky. The 5,355' summit of Mt. Ascension is Madison limestone. It is a rich destination point for rockhounds who consistently turn up an array primitive fossils. The great Missouri River cliffs 20 miles north of Helena that form the historic Gates of the Mountains also are Madison limestone.

The Missouri once surely flowed far above the canyon Lewis and Clark floated in the summer of 1805. But over time the river sawed its way through the resistant limestone. The result is one of the most beautiful canyons in the region. Mountain goats share the cliffs with bald eagles and rare peregrine falcons. The earthwork sediment of the Pleistocene-epoch Glacial Lake

Built in 1885, the Lewis and Clark County Courthouse was graced by four corner clock towers until the October earthquakes 50 years later. RICK GRAETZ

Great Falls' flooding of the canyon still can be read in the rock.

Historians contend that a journal entry by Meriwether Lewis on July 19, 1805 describes the limestone cliffs of what we call the Gates of the Mountains as appearing to bar passage to the Pacific. But because of the description of "black granite" in the entry, some Montana geologists believe the "true" gates Lewis described are several miles north.

The Madison limestone on Mt. Ascension is analogous to a big river that sweeps across the heads of Nelson, Grizzly, Oro Fino and Dry gulches, climbs over the top of Mt. Ascension and roars off to the southeast.

There is a peculiar architectural symmetry to mountain making. Why isn't Madison limestone found on the north slopes in contortions that mirror its course on the

The scenic overlook east of MacDonald Pass on the Continental Divide offers this view of the Prickly Pear Valley, with Helena mostly hidden by the range in the middle distance. RICK GRAETZ

south slopes? It is as if the Madison limestone was systematically washed off the north face of the foothills by those paltry creeks that must have once reigned as torrents, carrying the eroded hills like backfill into the valley and beyond.

Geologists know the Prickly Pear Valley is the product of erosion, too. And that Helena sits on the flank of a dome that once capped the valley from Marysville to York. Consider that the erosion has been so significant and thorough that the summit of the dome is now the valley itself. Erosion has made the dome a bowl and the bowl is presently cut from the core of the dome—some of the oldest sedimentary rock in Montana.

The hundreds of millions of years of strata that once insulated the ancient Precambrian mudstone—the easily recognizable white sheets of

limestone and other rocks—can now be seen in the city only on the bluffs of Mt. Helena. Beyond the city, the hills to the south and the flanks of the Big Belts to the north, and the Spokane Hills, also exhibit eroded limestone that once uniformly stretched across the valley like a bed sheet.

The Madison sea subsided and left Helena dry. The following age is distinguished by sand deposits of Pennsylvanian and Permian time. There follows a gap of time with no rock of ages in Helena. Once you dive into geology, considering spans of time can get eerie. Dr. James Hutton, an 18th century geologist and the patron saint of the modern science, at the risk of Christian sacrilege, decided in 1785 that the earth could not possibly have been created in 4004 BC, then the accepted belief. Hutton concluded the earth's age was entirely incomprehen-

sible. He said there was "no vestige of a beginning and no prospect of an end."

Scientists have brushed off the Helena-area gap following Pennsylvanian time. One Helena geological surveyor wrote: "After the deposition of the materials [of Pennsylvanian time] there is a gap in the recorded geologic history of the immediate region." And then plunged coldly into Cretaceous time.

But the gap lasted 140 million years. It encompassed three geologic periods—parts of the Permian, the Triassic and parts of the Jurassic. It was a time of erosion and apocryphal mass extinction but it could be argued that the gap marks the most significant time in Helena's geologic history.

In Permian time much of North America was dry; Montana was coastal and portions of the sea were actually present in the southern part of Montana. In Triassic time, the first block of the Mesozoic Era, a sea extended north from Utah and covered portions of southwest Montana, but the

period ended with Helena as a low-lying land surface. In the Jurassic, Helena remained coastal until midway through the period, when the sea spread across the land before withdrawing again. Near the end of the Jurassic, dinosaurs roamed central Montana in and around a fossil-rich swampland as vast as the Florida Everglades. The dinosaurs especially enjoyed the north periphery of the swamp where their bones are still being exhumed.

But through these ages, Helena appeared to remain on a calm, low-lying coastal landmass that extended from Siberia to New Mexico. And it has been theorized that, through a quirk of geology, that rough coast has outlined the course of the Great North Trail for more than 200 million years. The trail, a prehistoric migratory passage littered with the debris of evolution, has drawn paleontologists to it since the 1870s. There is something to be said about the fact that Helena's convenient proximity to the trail and the trail's offspring—the Old

North Trail of the Blackfeet Indians, the Nez Perce Hunting Trail, the Bozeman Trail, the Salt Lake Road, the Mullan Road, the railroads, the great cattle trails from Texas and our modern highways— has contributed more to Helena's existence than the mere discovery of gold.

The Prickly Pear Valley itself has been called a "transit zone" by historians. The valley actually connects the Missouri River's north-south travel with the geologic basins and faults

between the Rocky Mountains that provide an easy east-west travel route.

There may be no vestige of beginning in the rock, but the information stored as in a time capsule in the first 12,000 feet of Helena's sedimentary rock suggests a flat land that invited the sea for several eternities and waited several more for its return. The area has turned mountainous, yet it still awaits the sea. In late-Cretaceous time, Helena was in a spot on the globe turning

87

itself inside out with cataclysmic effect. A thick welt of volcanoes emerged like a whip-stroke on a bull's flank. The welt reached from Yellowstone, through the Elkhorn Mountains, to Augusta. The crumpling, rippling earth spewed its molten rock in an overture of violent eruptions in the Elkhorns. Several thousand feet of volcanic rocks east of Boulder, and evidence of lava flows in Livingston and at the mouth of the Little Prickly Pear canyon at Wolf Creek, help to measure the volcanoes' magnitude.

Classic volcanic cones must have developed in the Elkhorns along with the "Ancestral Rockies" but the mountains were so deeply eroded in Tertiary time their numbers only can be imagined. In places the lava formations were lifted vertical to the crumpling earth as the creation of the Rocky Mountains began.

In Montana's late-Cretaceous rock, bones of dinosaurs that cruised the river bottoms to the northeast are not rare. But around Helena most of the rock of that age has been cooked by magma and evidence of the giant reptiles is scarce.

After the end of Cretaceous time, however, there are no more signs of dinosaurs. None anywhere. The Cretaceous-to-Tertiary fence marks the extinction of the dinosaur, flying reptiles, sea reptiles, many species of fish and countless other lifeforms. The event is known as the Cretaceous Extinction and the most dramatic theory maintains that it was caused by a six-mile-wide asteroid hurled through space and time to meet the earth and explode with the unholy force of untold atomic bombs. A thick cloud of debris created its own atmosphere, affecting light and heat. The earth was engulfed in a climate like that of the theoretical "nuclear winter" and nearly every living thing was killed.

All of late-Cretaceous to early-Tertiary time was marked by cataclysm. The Boulder

Batholith, an enormous glob of once-molten rock that tried mightily to boil to the surface, has its beginnings about this time.

The formation is mostly granite now, as hard as it was once hot, and stretches from Helena to beyond Butte. As the magma tried to boil to the surface it cooked and transformed the sedimentary shales, limestones and sandstones it touched south of Helena. The magma, like a river, searched for easy passage. (If magma reaches the surface via a volcano, geologists then call it lava.)

The batholith magma was hot enough to bore through and melt weakened primeval surface deposits. Ascending from the earth's crust, magma squeezed itself through any deposit that allowed its intrusion until it backed up, as if by a dike, in molten subterranean lakes that engulfed adjacent rocks and cooled over millions of years in globs and clusters.

Quartz vains slashed the granite. The ancient Greeks thought it a product of super-

The fossil-filled Madison Limestone of Refrigerator Canyon once was the bottom of a tropical sea. JOHN REDDY

cooled ice and Pliny the Elder, who perished under Vesuvius, thought quartz could be found only "in places where the winter snow freezes with the greatest intensity."

Whether early Montana gold prospectors were acquainted with the classics or not, they did know quartz. Quartz meant gold and the batholith, with its great granitic humps and slabs laid bare through erosion, was as good as money in the bank. A 70-million-year-old bank, stuffed like thousands of rocky mattresses with deposits. The batholith yielded its first withdrawal hardly a century ago. But it retains its secrets.

Geology. It is a cosmic Rubik's cube and few people ever get it straight. But not for lack of trying. Pity the poor geologist trying to explain the origin of the 70-million-year-old Boulder Batholith. The plate tectonic theory says the magma lake should be 100 miles west, nearer to the Bitterroot Mountains' Idaho Batholith.

Still, although no one knows why the Boulder batholith is where it is, we do know that all of the Elkhorn Mountains' volcanic rocks were erupted from it. Geologists believe the Boulder Batholith supplied the fuel for a huge Elkhorn volcano, like the resurgent caldera in Yellowstone National

Park that the slow rhythms of earth have gently brought round another 600,000 years, making us on schedule now for its regular destructive belch.

Not Vesuvius and Mt. St. Helens combined could match its potential for destruction.

Early in the Tertiary, the eroded surface of western Montana was uplifted as the grinding western edge of the North American Plate was slowly creeping up the worn flanks of the Pacific Ocean crustal plate that continued to dig itself a deeper trench. Layered slabs of sedimentary rock slipped to the east like a deck of cards fanned and half-flipped in preparation for a magic trick. The results are most dramatic along the upward-tilted Rocky Mountain Front.

In places where the sedimentary rock was less orderly the uplifting earth folded, stretched, jerked, heaved and finally buckled and broke to create more of the Rocky Mountains.

Because Helena so pleasantly lies on the south side of the great dome uplift, in part created by these events, it is easy to ignore the ever-present threat of a violent earthquake. The dome itself is crumpled

from mountain-making and the sedimentary rock is faulted—broken. Inactive faults cut across areas south and east of Helena. Three major active faults lie north of town, in the valley. They are the Bald Butte Fault, the Iron Mine Fault and the Helena Valley Fault, the northernmost major fault in the Rockies.

The Prickly Pear, or Helena, Valley is on the northern end of an active seismic zone that extends south through Yellowstone National Park, Salt Lake City and on to Nevada. Between 1903 and 1935 more than 60 minor earthquakes were recorded. Minor quakes have continued to gently rock this town.

The zone is known as the Intermountain Seismic Belt and is another misplaced square on the cosmic Rubik's Cube geologists seek to solve.

Beginning on October 3, 1935, more than 1,200 earthquakes were recorded in 80 days. The first destructive shock occurred October 12. It lasted seven seconds and was followed by 60 aftershocks over six days. Then the most violent earthquake struck for 30 seconds or longer and again on October 31, after more than 500 aftershocks, Helena experienced another severe quake that resulted in additional property damage, suffering and loss of life. The violent and destructive quakes prompted a short-lived attempt during Montana's next legislative session to move the capital from Helena to more settled ground.

The Indians explained the frequent quakes and shimmers through myth and magic. We can do little better today. Active seismic belts normally mark the boundaries of the earth's crash-car crustal plates. The Intermountain

N.P. LAND OFFICE
HELENA QUAKE
OCT 12-27 1935

JORUD
PHOTO
246

Seismic Belt marks no such boundary. The fault in the Prickly Pear Valley southeast of town, generally to blame for the violent quakes of the 1930s, is best described as a descendant of the historic earthquakes and volcanism that have been a part of Montana for 50 million years.

Helena is vulnerable to earthquakes because it sits on the soft valley sediments that fill the eroded dome. Geologists Dave Alt and Donald W. Hyndman, in *Roadside Geology of Montana,* have come up with an apt Prickly Pear Valley simile to show how and why the valley is so vulnerable. Think of a

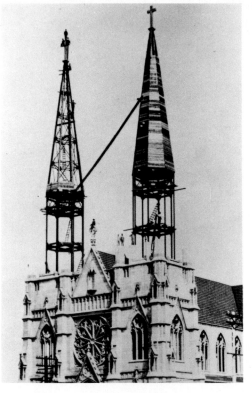

large bowl of pudding; the bowl is bedrock and the pudding is the soft sediment of the valley. Imagine sharply rapping the edge of the bowl to simulate an earthquake. When struck, the bowl jumps, rocks and stops, but the pudding wiggles in recurring waves before settling. Much of Helena is now built on the pudding.

A large part of the floor of the Prickly Pear Valley is underlain by Tertiary "lake-bed" deposits composed of light hues of clay sandwiched by sand and gravel. Along the gentle slope between Helena and East Helena, the beds are fine-grained volcanic ash—"tuff"—weathered and

Top: *Below MacDonald Pass.*
RICK GRAETZ
Left: *Construction workers pose on St. Helena Cathedral, around 1912, giving scale to the spires and the crosses atop them.* COURTESY JEAN BAUCUS

hardened, yet still soft and porous.

Much of the wrinkled valley floor is covered by sands, silts and mud (alluvium) brought down by rivers and streams in floods from Pleistocene (less than 1.8 million years ago) to recent age.

The alluvium consists of broad, gently sloping alluvial fans formed by Prickly Pear and Tenmile creeks and other valley streams. Each fan contains fragments of rocks present in the drainage basin of the stream that formed the deposit. In every case the alluvial deposits are coarse-grained and thicker near the mountains and finer and thinner in the lower parts of the valley. They were deposited over folded and eroded Tertiary "lakebeds" and older rocks. Similar lakebed valleys are cradled throughout the intermountain region of western Montana. Some geologists theorize that the Prickly Pear Valley was once a "ponded" river valley, possibly caused by a combination of local uplifts that created a backwash lake and lava flows that effectively impounded the historic southward drainage systems.

The dammed lake waters spilled northward, and created a river searching for a course of lower elevation. Erosion eventually helped the river cut a passage through the uplifts. This created canyons since eroded as low as or lower than the valley floor, which ultimately drained the lake.

These lake-spawned rivers flowing from broad valley to broad valley via narrow canyons are typical of the Missouri River canyons between Three Forks and Toston, and the Gates of the Mountains. The course of the Missouri was further altered during the Ice Age, when the glacier crept into Montana and formed the Missouri's course across Montana's northern plains.

SELECTED BIBLIOGRAPHY

Alt, Dave. "The Madison Limestone: Our Local Rock of Ages." *Montana Magazine,* March-April 1987.

___, and Donald W. Hyndman. *Roadside Geology of Montana.* Missoula: Mountain Press Publishing Company, 1986.

Alwin, John, A. *Western Montana: A Portrait of the Land and Its People.* Helena: Montana Magazine, Inc., 1983.

Baucus, Jean. *Gold in the Gulch.* Helena: Bar Wineglass, 1981.

Beer, Ralph. "Holding to the Land: A Rancher's Sorrow." *Harper's,* September 1985.

Borland, Hal. *Homeland: A Report from the Country.* Philadelphia: Lippincott, 1969.

Berg, Richard B. and Ray H. Breuninger, comps. *Guidebook of the Helena Area, West-Central Montana.* Montana Bureau of Mines and Geology, Special Publication 95, 1987.

Campbell, William C. *From the Quarries of Last Chance Gulch: A "News History" of Helena and Its Masonic Lodges, Compiled from the Files of Helena Newspapers,* 2 vols. Helena: Montana Record Publishing, 1951-52.

Cunningham, Bill. "Gates of the Mountains: Fossil Beds, Wild Flower Wonders." *Montana Magazine,* Nov.-Dec. 1984.

Cushman, Dan. *The Great North Trail.* New York: McGraw-Hill, 1966.

___. *Montana—The Gold Frontier.* Great Falls: Stay Away, Joe Publishers, 1973.

Davis, Les. "A Thousand Winters Ago." *Montana Outdoors,* March-April 1986.

Ehrlich, Gretel. "Letters to an Architect." *Northern Lights,* March-April 1986.

Gaff, James R., comp. *Historic Helena: An Early-Day Photographic History of Montana's Scenic Capital City.* Helena: Home Building Loan Association, 1964.

Harrington, John W. *Dance of the Continents: Adventures with Rocks and Time.* Los Angeles: J.P. Tarcher, Inc., 1983.

Harrison, Jim. *The Theory and Practice of Rivers.* Seattle: Wall Press, 1987.

Helena Board of Trade. *Helena Illustrated, Capital of the State of Montana: A History of the Early Settlement and the Helena of Today.* Minneapolis, Minn.: Pioneer Publishers, 1890.

Historical Research Associates. *Helena's South-Central Area: A Historical Survey.* Missoula: H.R.A., 1975.

Howard, Joseph Kinsey. *Montana High, Wide and Handsome.* Lincoln: University of Nebraska Press, 1983.

"How Helena Gets Its Name," *Helena Daily Independent,* January 27, 1910.

Jacobson, H.L., D.L. Byrd, and C. Jiusto. *Helena: A Historic City.* Helena, Mont., 1982.

Ide, A. W., and W.D. Rumsey, comp. *Helena, Montana: Its Past, Present and Future.* New York: South Publishing, 1894.

Langford, N.P. *Vigilante Days and Ways.* Reprint, Missoula: Montana State University Press, 1957.

McPhee, John. *Basin and Range.* New York: Farrar, Straus, Giroux, 1981.

Malone, Michael, and Richard Roeder. *Montana: A History of Two Centuries.* Seattle: University of Washington Press, 1976.

Meloy, Mark. "The Elkhorns: An Elegant Island of Mountains Tests a New Kind of Wild Land Protection Based on Wildlife Management." *Montana Magazine,* May-June 1982.

Munson, Lyman E. "Pioneer Life in Montana," *Contributions to the Montana Historical Society,* 1904.

Paladin, Vivian A., and Jean Baucus. *Helena: An Illustrated History.* Norfolk, VA: Donning Publishers, 1983.

Robinson, Willard B. "Helena's Fabulous Business Blocks." *Montana the Magazine of Western History,* Winter 1968.

Reese, Rick, ed. *Montana's Mountain Ranges,* rev. ed. Helena: Montana Magazine, Inc., 1986.

Silliman, Lee. "The Hangman's Tree." *Montana the Magazine of Western History,* Autumn 1978.

Skidmore, Bill. *Treasure State Treasury: Montana Banks, Bankers & Banking 1964-1984.* Helena: Montana Bankers Association, 1985.

Smurr, J.W. "Afterthoughts on the Vigilantes." *Montana the Magazine of Western History,* April 1958.

Walter, David. "Historical Survey: The Prickly Pear Valley, North of Helena, Montana [1980]." Vertical Files, Montana Historical Society Library.

RICK GRAETZ